Pick Up The Phone
Your Better Life Is Calling

How To Make Yourself A Priority
And Value Your Time

ISBN 979-8-9893023-0-7

Designed by Dericia J. Turner
Edited by Candice R. Jones, Giselle S. Mays, and Dericia J. Turner

We hope you enjoyed this book from Hartwell Ridge Publishing. Our goal
is to provide high quality, thought-provoking products and books to assist
you on your journey to your better life. *We do not proclaim to be medical doctors
or therapists. You should seek professional services for medical help. This book is a matter
of opinions and suggestions only.* Don't forget to try our challenges at the back of
the book. Let them inspire you to create your own. Tag us and subscribe to
all of our social media platforms.

Visit us on the web!

www.pickupthephone.com

This book is dedicated to my wife
who motivates me to live my better life everyday.

Table of Contents

Introduction

Everything costs and everything costs everything. What price are you willing to pay for what you say you want? If you want everything, and I mean everything — I'm talking Lamborghinis, mansions, yachts, and exotic vacations — you can have it. The question is, are you willing to pay the price to get it? You can live this life, but do you believe it's possible? Why do we doubt ourselves and what we are capable of before we even try? The answer is in this book. It's the reason you picked it up--you know your life should be better. How much better can it get? You'd be surprised. The hardest part of this journey is going to be believing it can happen to you. It won't be easy, but I guarantee you it will be worth it. I am going to help you learn how to make yourself a priority and value your time. It is my hope that your experience while reading this book unlocks a part of you that was hidden away, just waiting for a chance to grab the light and lead you into your better life. I'm supposed to say a better life but why would you want *a better life* when you can have *your better life*. I don't care what kind of life you are currently living. You have no idea how much better it can be if you get out of your own way. This is not the type of book you read; this is the type of book you *must* live. If you become one of the few who can utilize every method and technique laid out in the following pages, you will become limitless, and I'll meet you at the top. If you can only utilize some of the methods and techniques in the following pages that's okay, I hope you are able to live your better life. The life that you choose. It took decades to program you into the person you are currently but if you take action with intention, you can reprogram yourself a lot faster than you even know.

Chapter 1

Pick up the Phone: *or Don't*

I am about to show you how your life functions exactly like your phone. Do you even want to talk on the phone right now, or are you preoccupied because something else has your full attention? Most of the time, when we hear our phone ring, we pick up the phone, but on those occasions when we let it ring it's usually because we don't want to be interrupted. I would argue this is how most people live their lives, not wanting to be interrupted.

Your conscious mind will always report to the subconscious mind. Let's define the conscious mind and the subconscious mind before we go any further. Your conscious mind makes decisions you are aware of. Your subconscious mind is the part of the mind that's not fully aware but influences every action you take and every feeling you have. In short, your conscious mind does the thinking, and your subconscious mind makes the decision. Let's look at someone who wants to go back to school and get a degree they missed out on. Their conscious mind knows a degree would probably increase their earning potential and ultimately lead them to a better life than they are currently living. Why don't most people go back to school? It is because your subconscious mind knows that when you go back to school and get your degree, it will be replaced with new programming. It reports back to the conscious mind that school is boring, expensive, time consuming, and probably won't pay off; therefore, you never act. The key word I want you to focus on is programming. We like to think we are in control of our lives, but we aren't. We are merely programs running on the operating systems we have downloaded. I will prove it to you with this next question. What's your favorite color? Pretty easy question to answer, right? You probably didn't even need to think about the answer. Why is that your favorite color? This question required a little thought right. You probably don't know why you picked that color to be your favorite, and if you do, it is probably tied to something sentimental from your past. You didn't pick your favorite color; it was chosen for you by your subconscious mind along with everything else in life you think, do, or have.

If I were to ask you, what does the ideal version of yourself look like? You would say something like they are fun, charismatic, outgoing, successful, well-dressed, enthusiastic about life, in shape, well-educated, etc. If I were to ask you, what type of life does the ideal version of yourself live? You would say they drive a luxury car, live in a big house, wouldn't punch a clock, take vacations to exotic destinations, and have millions of dollars in the bank. I'm sure as you read the last two sentences, your mind did one of two things. You either pictured yourself with all or some of those things and character traits I just listed, or you told yourself I could never become all those things. Your mind immediately either accepted or rejected the idea of your better life.

Why? Your subconscious mind is designed for self-preservation. What exactly does this mean? I am saying your subconscious mind is trying to do its best to keep everything the same because that's it's job. Your subconscious mind is trying to protect you from yourself. This is why you immediately reject the idea of your better life and settle for the one that you currently have. Let us take one aspect of your better life I mentioned in the previous paragraph, such as being fit. We know it's not as simple as saying if you want to lose weight, then lose weight. There are things you will have to do in order to achieve this goal. You'll need to exercise regularly and eat healthier. What does exercising regularly mean? Does this mean every day or every other day? What type of exercises should I be doing? Should I do yoga or walk around the block? Should I lift weights, or should I focus on cardio, or should I be doing all of these things? I know I should be eating healthier. I need to stop eating fast food, drinking sodas, and eating junk food. I need to eat more green foods, add more color to my plate, drink more water, and eat more fruit. Your subconscious mind processed all of that from the words loose weight and told you it was too much, so why bother doing any of it? Let's take another aspect of your better life I mentioned previously, such as taking exotic vacations. If I were to ask you what type of person takes exotic vacations, you would probably say a person who has their finances in order. What does this look like? They would obviously have disposable income, which would mean they are financially stable and smart with their money. They would know how to save and not spend. They would be disciplined with their money habits. When you read the previous statements, your mind did one of two things: Your subconscious mind said you are none of those things, so don't get your hopes up of ever becoming that, or your conscious mind told you to become all of those thing in order to live your better life. Let's say the conscious part of your mind wins this battle, and now you are motivated to become a better version of yourself and start living your better life. The moment you start to go after your better life, your subconscious mind says you will never be able to change this much. You realize how hard it will be to accomplish these things, and you retreat back to the life you know and feel comfortable with. At that point, your subconscious mind says I told you so. Just stick with me, and we'll be okay. Why does this happen? As I stated earlier in this chapter, your subconscious mind is designed for self-preservation. We have all experienced this before.

So, how do you live the life you want to live and reprogram your mind to do what you know you should be doing in order to live your better life? With intentionality, meaning that when you are faced with a decision, you must immediately choose the one that advances you forward. Do not give your subconscious mind a chance to even reject the idea. I know it's easier said than done, but you can do it. Let's go back to the example of losing weight. Instead of thinking about all of the things that need to be done to lose weight, just start with one thing and commit to it consistently. Start by eating one piece of fruit daily. That's it. Start with something you know you can do and follow through on it. If you eat one piece of fruit every day for 30 days, you will find yourself on a new path to losing weight. What will soon happen is that you will add to your fitness routine because this is exactly what you have started — a new routine. Next, add to your routine and challenge yourself to walk around the block for twenty to thirty minutes every other day for thirty days. The only way to reprogram your mind is to develop new habits to replace the old ones. The easiest way to do this is to make one habit at a time. Pick something you know you can follow through with. If you know you should read more books, then read more books. Here's how you do it: Tell yourself, "I am going to read two pages from a book every day for thirty days and commit to it." By the end of day thirty, I promise you will be reading more than two pages a day.

Imagine that every day you wake up, you get a phone call from your better life. Most people will not pick up the phone and have this conversation. I believe the reason is because our better life is going to ask us to do things we don't want to do. Like when your friend calls and asks you to take them to work. You take them, and then what happens? They call you the next day and need another ride to work. If they continue to ask you for a ride to work at some point, you will tell them, "I can't take you anymore. You need to find another ride to work." Even if they are offering you gas money, you still don't want to do it. If they continue to call you at some point, you will stop picking up the phone and start ignoring their calls. We do this to our better life every day. Every day you have the opportunity to create your better life, but your subconscious mind tells you the life you're living is good enough. To create anything, you must take action, and as we've discussed earlier, your subconscious mind doesn't want to take any action other than the ones it knows. This is why you have the habits you have. You have repeated the same action enough times that your mind does it automatically. This is why you have to be intentional about setting up new habits that will serve you and advance you forward in life rather than falling deeper into the self-destructive habits we all have.

The best way to be intentional is to develop your awareness of these self-destructive habits that don't serve you. Self-awareness is the key to unlocking your better life. For example, a doctor can tell a patient they are very overweight and unhealthy, and they are going to be diabetic if they don't change their eating habits. This patient was probably already aware of what the doctor said before the visit but chose to ignore all the signs their body was giving them. They will most likely leave the doctor's office and continue the same routine they had before speaking with their doctor, continuing their self-destructive habits until they are forced to change. Let's take the same patient, but this time the doctor says you are now diabetic, your A1C level is at 8%, and you must take several insulin shots every day for the rest of your life. You could be at risk of having a stroke or having parts of your body amputated if you do not make significant changes in your eating habits. Your level of self-awareness around food would change dramatically. Every time you picked up food to put into your mouth, you would be self-aware of the potential positive or negative effects this food would have on your body. The doctor's words would either cause you to take action and create a new lifestyle that would benefit your overall health going forward, or not. Even when faced with dire circumstances that require people to change for the sake of living, some people still choose not to change and instead choose death. Why is this? It is because your sub-conscious mind is programmed for self-preservation, even at the expense of you. This is how powerful your subconscious mind is. It can literally kill you. That's how strong your programming can become. It's no different than cigarette smokers who smoke even though the box says it will give you cancer. This is why you should always initiate the change you want to see in your life before life forces you to change.

Being intentionally aware is the first step to living your better life. My definition of intention is a wish that one wants to carry out. My definition of being aware is having knowledge of a situation. We can define being intentionally aware as knowing what you want to do, why you are doing it, and how you are going to get it done. If you can be become intentionally aware in more areas of your life, the more things you can reprogram and change. Reprogramming your subconscious mind is like having a bucket filled with water, and there's sand at the bottom of the bucket. The bucket represents your whole mind, and the sand represents the negative thoughts that are always in your subconscious mind. Let the water be the conscious thoughts you deliberately place in your mind. How do you get the sand (negative thoughts) out of the bucket (your mind) without picking up the bucket and dumping everything out? You will need to flush out the sand. How do you do that? You will need to run new water (conscious thoughts) into the bucket to get the sand out. You must make sure the new water you put into the bucket is coming into it with enough force to reach the bottom of the bucket and remove the sand at the bottom. When we do this, something is going to happen. We are going to make a mess. Water and sand are going to splatter everywhere. The second you try to reprogram your subconscious mind, you are going to make a mess of the life you are currently living because you are disrupting the comfort zone you have grown accustomed to. This is the point where most people cut the water off, go back to their lesser lives, and stop trying to live their better life. We don't realize how much of our lives we need to clean up until we attempt to live better lives. You will soon find yourself wanting to go back to the old version of yourself because that life was easier. This is when

19

you will realize how powerful your subconscious mind is, but I want you to know you have a cheat code you probably aren't using. *Your cheat code is goals.* I will discuss this in depth in Chapter 7.

Another reason you don't pick up the phone and live your better life is because you are inherently or naturally lazy. It's not your fault, times have changed. There was a time when pretty much nobody was lazy, and we all worked on farms all day, and the kids walked for miles to school, but those times are gone. The times you currently live in have programmed you to seek comfort and ease. In the kitchen, people went from cooking in ovens to microwaves to air fryers and pressure cookers. We went from fast food and TV dinners to calling Uber Eats, so we don't even have to leave our house to get the food from our favorite restaurants. We went from having to watch a show when it aired to TiVo and DVR to streaming whatever you want whenever you want. Our entire lives have been shaped to seek comfort and ease. You can even buy an electric car that will chauffeur you around while you watch TV. The times that we are living in now are so easy that we exert all our energy at work and have none left for ourselves afterwards. You want to pick up the phone for your better life, but when you see how hard it will be to change, you give up before you even start. Technology has made our lives extremely easy to live day to day, but while it has made our lives easier, technology has made our minds weaker. Every ad, commercial, video, song, TV show, and billboard are all programming us in one way or another daily to be consumers and not creatives. Your creative space is just outside of your comfort zone — on the other side of the mess you make when you leave your comfort zone. Most of us never get to the creative space because we turn back too early.

When you were a child, you lived in your creative space and thrived in it. You could play in your room by yourself and imagine all sorts of things that would keep you entertained all day. All you had was creativity and imagination. You can give a 3-year-old an empty box, and they will turn it into an airplane or a fort. This is because they haven't been programmed for complacency yet. This will happen once they start school. This is where the real programming begins, but this book isn't about how school programs you to fit in. It's about breaking all the programs that are holding you back from standing out and living your better life. To do this, we must revisit our childhood to remember what it was like to be a free spirit, to remember what it was like to use your imagination every day when you thought the world was full of possibilities. It still is. At the end of the day, we are all just children pretending to be adults. We are just mimicking how we think adults should walk, talk, and act. I want you to stop right here and take 60 seconds to travel back in time and speak to your 10-year-old self and give them advice. What would you say? Did you do it? You would say something like, take school more seriously, don't stop reading books, don't play video games so much, respect your parents more than you do, spend more time developing your talents and skills, don't quit when it gets hard, always save your money, and the list goes on. Truthfully, couldn't you tell your present-day self most of these same things?

Why is it easy for people to tell others what they should be doing but hard for people to tell themselves what needs to be done? The reason is because if I tell myself I need to do better I have to take action, and this means leaving the comfort zone that I have created. As we've discussed before, when I leave my comfort zone, I make a mess of my previous life, and this is where your ego gets bruised. I would define your ego as the way you feel about yourself or your self-esteem. Every time you tell yourself you are going to do something, and you don't follow through, your ego takes a hit. If your ego takes enough hits it will run and hide, and so will you. The reason you don't pick up the phone for your better life is because you know every lie you've ever told yourself, which is why you don't trust yourself. You told yourself you were going to quit doing something you knew you shouldn't be doing or start doing things you know you should be doing, and you didn't. So rather than lie to yourself anymore, you choose

22

to ignore your better life and not even try. If this is you, then I would like to take this opportunity to tell you that no matter how successful you become in life, you will be fighting with your ego for as long as you are alive, so you might as well join the fight.

Your ego, or self-esteem, plays a major role in your perspective on life. It will determine whether you are a glass half empty or a glass half full type of person. If you see the glass as half empty, you are right; it is half empty. If you see the glass as half full, you are right; it is half full. The thing about perspective is that it is subjective. It is yours. You determine it. The way to become successful and live your better life is to always try to look at the glass as half full. This will be hard to do if you have been programmed to have a half-empty perspective, but you can change your perspective if you try. The best and easiest way to start doing this is to ask yourself better questions. For example, if you got laid off from your job because of budget cuts, you might say, why did they have to lay people off? Couldn't the CEO and corporate managers take pay cuts? Why aren't they being laid off? What am I going to do now? This is the glass half-empty approach. The glass half full approach is to be intentionally aware of what is happening to you and deliberately place positive thoughts where the negative thoughts would dwell. A better question to ask would be: What do I want to do now that I am a free agent? When I update my resume, what skills can I add that I have gained from my previous place of work? What friends can I call to help me find new employment?

I want you to notice something about the two types of people I just mentioned. If you are a half-empty person, you are living your life from the past to the present. Every question you ask is negative and about things that you cannot change. If you are a half-full person, every question is about what you plan to do next, and you are living your life from the present to the future. We all fall into one of these two categories. This is probably one of the easiest programs we can change right away in our lives. The key is to be aware that you are looking at the glass as half empty instead of half full. Immediately start asking yourself questions that will advance you rather than hold you back. **Your better life is ahead of you, not behind you.**

What does your better life look like?

List 5 things you need to stop doing in order to live your better life

1.

2.

3.

4.

5.

List 5 things you need to start doing in order to live your better life

1.

2.

3.

4.

5.

Chapter 2

Calling ID: *Who's Calling?*

Some of you may be old enough to remember when most people had caller IDs on their phones. What caller ID allows you to do is screen calls and not answer calls from unknown numbers. It would tell you the name of every person who was calling you. Nowadays, most phones don't tell you who's calling unless you have that specific number saved in your phone under a contact name. We all have a list of contacts we have programmed into our phones, so when someone calls us, their name will appear and we will know exactly who it is. Some people even have different ring tones associated with different people, so they know who is calling before they even look at their phone.

Let's be honest, if you get a phone call from a number you don't recognize, you probably won't answer it, but if you do the conversation usually starts like this. "Hello?" And they respond by saying, "Can I speak to _____?" The very next thing almost everyone says is, "Who is this?" Why is this the universal response we have when answering a phone call when we don't know who is calling? It is because our minds do not operate well when we have uncertainty about something. When we use phrases like I'm really stressed out right now, I'm feeling really depressed, or I'm so frustrated, it is almost always because we have uncertainty around an aspect of life we feel like we aren't in control of. If you get up every day and follow the exact same routine you did the day before and the day before that, then you start to think you are in control of your life because it has become predictable.

The reason you feel frustrated, depressed, or stressed is because your subconscious mind has programmed you to think, act, and do the same things at the same time, every time, every day, and any disruption in that program will cause you to malfunction into one of those negative states of mind. Again, this programming all started when you were in school for thirteen years of your life. You got up before the sun came up and traveled to a building with fluorescent lights, where you were given work to do. They gave you a break during the middle of your day to eat, then you went back to doing more work. Every day you anxiously waited for the last bell to ring so you could leave to go enjoy the rest of your day, and to top it all off, they kept programming you even after school was over. How? They sent homework with you so you would not get too creative when you left school. You did this for thirty-two hours a week for thirteen years, from age five to 18. Let's compare that to your current daily routine. You get up before the sun and travel to a building with fluorescent lights, where you are given work to do. They give you a break during the middle of your workday so you can eat and have enough energy to get back to work. Every day, you wait for your shift to end so you can leave and enjoy the rest of your day. We do this for at least 40 hours a week. When it is time to retire, you have done this routine for around fifty years. That is roughly 104,000 hours of your life.

Once again, this book is not about how school programs you to fit in, but I do want you to know that you did not become this way overnight, and you won't fix it overnight either. However, you can change your life for the better. One of the first things you will need to do is visualize your better life. You need to see it in detail. What do you want to do? Who do you want to be? What do you want to have? Where do you want to go? What do you want to see? The reason you don't recognize what your better life looks like is because you have not thought about it enough to define it. You might say I want a brand new car, but that just says what you want without defining it, which is why you probably don't have a brand new car yet. This is your better life, so see it as clearly as you possibly can. Instead of saying I want a brand-new car, say I want a brand-new cherry red Chevrolet Camaro with a convertible top and black 19 inch rims, tinted windows and loud pipes in the back. See the difference? When you read the words brand-new car, there was no picture that popped into your mind because it wasn't defined. But when I said cherry red Chevrolet Camaro with a convertible top and black 19-inch rims, tinted windows, and loud pipes in the back, your mind automatically painted a vivid picture. The thing you need to realize is that I placed that thought in your mind, and you had no choice but to see it because I defined it for you. You can do this in your own life. Use your senses when you are defining what your better life looks like.

You don't always have to let other people and the world program you with thoughts they want you to think about. You can place thoughts in your mind and keep them there, and your world will start to take shape around those thoughts. Let me show you. Take a few seconds to think of something that you once wanted but now have. It could be your job, your spouse, your house, or any number of things in your life right now. How did you obtain it? By keeping the thought in your mind for so long, your subconscious mind had no choice but to take action towards obtaining what you wanted until you got it. This is how you are going to live your better life. You must define it in as much detail as possible and keep it at the forefront of your mind every day. If you do this, your subconscious mind will start to move you towards your better life, and your better life will start to move towards you. This is the law of attraction and how it works.

The easiest and fastest way to make this vision a reality in your life is to write it down. You must write it down for it to happen. Why? Because your mind can only bring into reality the thoughts that it can turn into images. You can only bring into reality things that your mind believes are possible. I'm sure you have heard the phrase "a picture is worth a thousand words." Let the words paint the picture. Even if you don't believe your better life is possible right now, take the time to think about it and write it down anyway. If you write down what it looks like and define it in as much detail as you can, you will find yourself visualizing this life. Your mind will begin to believe that you can have those things. The word I want you to focus on in the previous sentence is *believe*.

Belief is defined as accepting something as true. If you believe it is true, then you believe it is real. The reason we know what we believe is real is because we have already said previously that there are things you wanted in the past that you now have. Why? Because you believed you would get those things, and the truth is, it was yours the moment you believed it was, and you held your belief until it came into reality.

Everyone is always looking for shortcuts or the easy path to get to their better life and you will always hear people say there are no shortcuts or easy paths to a better life. They tell you it takes a lot of hard work, grinding, and sacrifice to get there, and while this may be true, I have found that there is a shorter route and an easy way to get there. You ready? The easiest way to pick up the phone and live your better life is to know where you are, know where you want to go, and start moving in that direction. Sounds easy enough, right? Like I said before, if you look at your life, this is exactly how you got anything in life you wanted up to this point so we know you can do it. Well, then why does it feel so hard to do? The reason it feels so hard to do is because you aren't programmed to want that life. You thought that was what you wanted, so you went after it whether it, was a degree, a girlfriend, or a car. You didn't think about how hard it would be to get it; you just went after it because your subconscious mind, told your conscious mind "I want that." Your programming had you running on cruise control until you obtained what you wanted. When you look back, it was probably easier than you thought it would be. It probably felt almost effortless.

The reason living your better life feels hard to do is because you are trying to get your conscious mind to tell your subconscious mind, I want that life, but your subconscious mind doesn't believe it yet. The subconscious part of your mind needs to see it to believe it which is why visualizing a better life is so important to the process of changing your life. The key is to visualize your better life in multiple ways. If you want a brand new car, then go to the dealership and look at it. Sit-in and test drive the new car you want. Get a feel for what it would be like to be behind the wheel. Get a printout of the specs of the car and its exact price from the dealership. If you want to own a home or buy a new house, then go to open houses on the weekend. If you want a two-story 4,000-square-foot house with a big yard in a certain neighborhood, find out what time the open house is and go walk through it. Imagine yourself living there. What do you like about the house, and what would you like to change once you move in? Do you want to add a pool to the backyard? Do you want to change the light fixtures? Really take in the experience as if you were going to put an offer on the house. Do this regularly to keep it at the forefront of your conscious mind.

Another way to take your visualization to another level is to practice meditation. The best time is at the beginning or end of your day. The end goal would be to get to the point where you are doing it to start and end your day to maximize the law of attraction. It only takes 5 to 15 minutes of your time. There are plenty of books on meditation, but I will give you a simple way to get started. You need to be in a room with no external distractions. Turn the light off, turn the TV off, and sit in one spot where you are comfortable and close your eyes. Focus on breathing in and out and relaxing your eyelids. When you do this, your mind will want to think about all kinds of things because one thing the mind cannot do is never have a thought. Just sit there and let those thoughts pass, and when you feel calm, start trying to visualize what you want. Ask yourself questions about the car. See yourself driving that car. What color is it? Can you smell the leather? Does it have a sunroof? You might not be able to see anything when you first try this, but that's okay. Most people think if they don't see anything, then they are doing it wrong, and this is not the case. I guarantee you that if you keep trying, you will get better at it, and the visualizations will get stronger. Meditation is a skill, and just like any skill, you must practice it to get better at it. If you stick with it, there will come a point where you will start to have vivid visualizations of your better life.

The best way I can describe it to you is at first, it's like looking up at the sky and seeing nothing but clouds, and then the sky

34

opens for a few seconds, and you can see the sun just before it's gone back behind the clouds. At first, you will not be able to have complete, vivid visualizations. It will be glimpses of your better life that come and go, but at some point, you will have a visualization that feels real. It will feel like an out-of-body experience, and you will feel like you are looking down on yourself being, doing, and having all the things your mind can imagine. If you write it down in detail, go touch it and visualize yourself having it on a regular basis. Your subconscious mind has no choice but to believe you really want these things, and it will begin to take action. It will move you toward the things you see yourself having, and it will feel like these things are starting to move towards you naturally. If you can write it down, visualize it, and go touch it, these three things will accelerate your journey towards your better life.

All these things help you recognize what your better life looks like and make it easier for you to pick up the phone because you know who is calling and what they want from you. The uncertainty that most people have about living a better life will turn into confidence for you to move forward. While most people have doubts about their future and are scared they might not achieve the things they say they want, you will have the confidence to know that it is already yours because you have seen yourself with these things already. If you can see it, then you can believe it, and you can believe it because you can see it. Visualization will create a continuous loop from your subconscious mind to your conscious mind and back to your subconscious mind. This will drastically increase your belief in what is possible for you. The best part is that you get to decide what your better life looks like. You finally get to be the person programming your life instead of the world programming you to want things that you really don't want but instead settle for. When you can do this, you have begun the process of reprogramming your subconscious mind.

The word I want you to focus on in the last sentence is process, because that is exactly what this is: a process. I would define a process as a series of actions or steps taken in order to achieve a particular end. You must understand that it will not happen overnight, but if you do this daily, you are constantly closing the gap between where you are and where you want to be. Your subconscious mind will actively seek out ways to achieve the outcome that you want, and you will start to notice different opportunities and ways to get there. Not only this, but your subconscious mind will also cause you to take action towards what you want, and it won't feel like you are forcing it. It will feel like it is all coming to you naturally. But the truth is, most people never even start the process.

I can't explain to you why this works, but I can try to

help you understand how it works. What kind of car do you have? We'll use a Chevy Malibu for this example. You probably never paid attention to how many Chevy Malibu's were on the road until you got one yourself, and then you began to see them everywhere all the time. You even notice the differences in the models from year to year compared to the model that you are driving. Why is this? Are there suddenly more Chevy Malibu's on the road? No, they've been there the entire time, but because your mind perceives this car to be important to you and because you see yourself in it every day, your mind now notices all the Chevy Malibu's around you. This is exactly what will happen to you when you start the process of re-programming your mind. You will start to notice opportunities that have been around you the entire time that you never noticed before.

One of the main reasons people become successful is because they know exactly what they want in life. They go after it and don't stop until they have reached their better life, and even then, they don't actually stop; they just put that same energy and effort into chasing down their next better life. It is a never-ending journey to see what you can become. Success is subjective, meaning no one can tell you what your success looks like. Only you get to determine what success looks like to you and how successful you want to become, but there are levels to success. The student who became a teacher, who then became a principal, who became an area director, who became the superintendent of the school district, who then became the chair of the state board of education, was nominated by the president of the United States to be the secretary of the U.S. Department of Education. It is up to you to determine what your better life looks like and chase it down with everything you have.

Living your better life is not going to be easy; it will be challenging, but that is where you build up the mental capacity to do what you have set out to do. If today I just dropped you into the seat of CEO at FedEx, you wouldn't have a clue what needed to be done or how it should be done. You would not have the experience or capacity to handle the position, and your failure would be guaranteed. This is why you have to go through the tough times of grinding it out and pushing past the doubt and uncertainty on your journey to living your better life. Not for what it will bring you, but because of what you will become in the process. One of the hardest parts of your journey will be starting and not giving up when you don't see immediate results. You must believe there is a better life for you and chase it down every day without fail. At some point, you will look up and find yourself at the destination of your choice.

Pick up the phone; your better life is calling you every day, and it is a lot better than the one you are currently living. When you realize your better life is like a Lego piece you can stack one on top of the other, you will go from feeling limited to feeling limitless. I will let you in on a little secret, the higher you go in life the easier it becomes to get the next Lego piece because all the competition is at the bottom. When you hear the phrase "it's lonely at the top," you picture a person who has everything they ever wanted but is alone and has no one to share it with. That is not what this phrase means. What this phrase means is that it is crowded at the bottom. When you reach the top, you will realize that there is no competition at the top; you have no peers because everyone is looking up to you. You will realize that you are your only competition. When successful people get to this point, they still don't stop, even though they can go no higher. They find another bottom to start from, pick up the phone again, and begin to chase down their next better life. That is why people like Elon Musk, who became the world leader in the EV market, said his next challenge is that he wants to go to outer space, and he started SpaceX. That is why Mark Zuckerberg, who became the leader in the social media space, said he wanted to create a digital world and started the metaverse. That is why people like Jeff Bezos, who started Amazon and became the number one online retailer, started Amazon Prime and now create TV shows and movies for people to stream. The only person who can limit where you go in life is you.

You must realize your power to be, do, and have anything you want in this life, within reason, of course. If you are 38 years old and want to play in the NBA, this is not within reason. Your body won't let you compete with 19-year-olds no matter how hard you try, but if you make it to the NBA and take care of your body, then you can keep playing to the age of 38 because you have been doing it for 19 years and have mastered the game. I want you to breakdown what I just said because it is important for you to get this. I'm not saying that a 38-year-old can't play in the NBA. What I am saying is that there are certain opportunities in life that come and go and will never come back again. The 38-year-old who wants to play in the NBA did not take advantage of his youth and missed an opportunity, and it will never come back around. This is why it is so important for you to start chasing down your better life today because there are opportunities waiting for you that you aren't even aware of, but they do have an expiration date.

Your better life that is calling you at 19 is not the same better life that is calling you at 38. This is why it is so crucial for you to first know there is a better life calling you every day, and secondly if you don't pick up the phone for that better life, it will stop calling. You won't even realize you have missed the opportunity because you didn't even know it existed. The good news is that when your better life has stopped calling you, there is always another better life calling, but you must pick up the phone to know what that better life looks like. The older you get, the harder it gets to pick up the phone. Why? Because the older you get, the more set in your ways you become. You become comfortable with the way things are and lose hope for how much better things could be.

When you get older and reflect on your life, you start to feel regret because you realize you could have done so much more in your life. You realize you had a lot of missed opportunities, and you know they aren't coming back around again. This is where some people experience a mid-life crisis. You must realize that feeling regret is okay. This means you are reflecting, and it gives you a chance to now look forward to your better life and not miss the next opportunity that may come your way. It gives you a chance to pick up the phone for your better life that is calling now and turn regrets into rewards. Some people don't ever check their voicemail, and no one can leave them messages because their mailbox is full. Sadly, this is how most people go through life, with automated programs running around doing the same thing at the same time with the same people in the same way every day. They are living the same day over and over again.

Don't let this be you. Break out of your current pro-gramming and pick up the phone for your better life every day. See what it is asking you to do. **When the unknown becomes known, you have nothing to fear but fear itself, and fear is just a figment of your imagination.**

First step to your better life

Write it down.

It's not real *until* you do

Close your eyes and envision your better life. *What do you see?*

- What type of career do you have? Where are you vacationing?

- How many square feet is your dream home? Is it a high-rise condo in the city or a big brick house in the suburbs?

- Describe the cars parked on your motor court. Are they exotic super cars, or luxury vehicles?

Chapter 3

Answer or Reject: *You get to choose*

When your phone rings, you are presented with two options: answer or reject the call, but there is also a third option you get to choose from, and that is to ignore the call. We look at who is calling, and we put the phone down and continue with what we were doing before we got the call. We neither answered nor rejected the call. When we answer the call, it is usually because we know who is on the other end of the phone trying to reach us. When we reject the call, it is because we don't want to talk to whoever is on the other end of the phone trying to reach us. When we ignore the call, it is usually because we don't want the person on the other end of the phone to know that we rejected the call. We know that if we hit reject, it will go straight to voicemail, and the person on the other end of the phone will know we rejected their call. If we let it ring, we think they will assume we are just busy and will call them back later. We usually ignore the call instead of rejecting it because we don't want the person calling to feel rejected. In some strange way, we feel like ignoring is better than rejecting, but they both produce the same outcome so what's the difference anyway? But there's also a fourth option we all have used before, which is answering and rejecting the call at the same time.

If it is someone important, like your boss, spouse, or the person you are dating, you will answer and then reject the call. You will pick up the phone and say something like, "Hey, can I call you back when I get done doing _____?" I would argue that most people who decide to go after their better life eventually start answering the phone this way when their better life calls. Let's take the previous example of the teacher who became the secretary of education. Remember how in chapter one I told you that your subconscious mind is designed for self-preservation and to seek comfort and ease? What most people would do is stop after becoming teachers. Why is this? It's because your new subconscious mind doesn't want to be replaced. It wants to stay in control by keeping everything the same. You set this goal for yourself, went after it, and achieved that desired goal. Now your subconscious mind says, "We can stay here forever. This place is not that bad. You have a steady paycheck, job security, and a pension for retirement." You convince yourself that because you might be doing better than others, this is a good place to stop.

The phrase I want you to focus on in the last sentence is 'doing better than others' because this thinking is what convinces you that where you are now is the finish line when it is actually just a checkpoint. I would define a checkpoint as the place along the route of a long-distance race where the time for each competitor is recorded. Your life is a long-distance race, and it doesn't end until it ends. Remember when I told you how it's crowded at the bottom and lonely at the top? This is why. How many teachers are there in the U.S.? At the time of writing this book, there were around 4,007,908 teachers in the U.S. There are just under 90,000 principals in the U.S. There are around 7,200 school district superintendents in the U.S. There are just over 2,550 area directors in the U.S. There are 50 chair positions on the state board of education, and there is one secretary of the U.S. Department of Education nominated by the president of the United States.

The best analogy for success I have heard I will credit to Myron Golden. He said success is like a rocket ship. In the beginning, it takes a tremendous amount of force and power just to get off the ground for take off as it starts rising towards the atmosphere. The ship will start shaking violently on the way up and feel like it is going to fall apart, so you hold on for dear life. At a certain height, the boosters will fall off because you don't need them anymore, and you will break through the atmosphere and start floating. The ship now uses no force and travels at a speed of 5 miles per second around the earth effortlessly. This is how success is going to look in your life. The beginning is always the hardest part, but the higher you go, the easier it gets. Most people just don't go high enough to find out how easy it is to get there and stay there.

The real key to getting to the top and staying there is to keep the momentum going and never let it stop. You should be going from your better life to your next better life until you reach the top. When you reach the top, you will find it was all worth it because the view is something most people never get to see. The feeling is one that most people never get to have, and you are one of the chosen ones who get to experience it. This is why people like Elon Musk, Mark Zuckerburg, and Jeff Bezos load up another rocket ship and do it again. Your average person would say, "Why are they working so hard? If I became a billionaire, I would sell my business and enjoy life. I would just do what I wanted, when I wanted, and how I wanted all the time."

They understand it's not about money but about growth and personal development. It's about challenging yourself to see what you can become. You have no idea how unlimited your potential is as a human being until you start to stack one better life on top of the other consistently without stopping. You must understand you are going to grow into your better life, not just magically appear there. The thing you need to know about growth is that nothing grows in a straight line. Growing into your better life is going to look more like a stock chart than a straight line. When a stock goes up, it will go up for a while, then there will be a small pullback. Next. it will go up some more, and then there will be another small pullback. It will continue to do this until it reaches its peak. You can't let the small pullback that is guaranteed to happen during your journey to the top throw you off and send you into a negative spiral where you quit and go back to the starting line.

This is why being intentionally aware of what you are doing every day is so important. If you surround yourself with as much positivity as you can, your subconscious mind will not have enough negativity to override the new program you are downloading. Read more positive self-help books like this one. Listen to motivational speakers instead of music on your ride to and from work or while you are working out. Only watch content that will inspire you along your journey. Watch videos of people telling their stories about how they once were where you are and are now doing what you want to do. By doing this daily, you will be able to recognize when you have gotten into a slump and will be able to shake it off and get right back on the path to your better life.

This is why you must pick up the phone for your better life every day, because the moment you stop picking up the phone, you are going to go backwards fast and find yourself right back in that same negative subconscious state of mind. Your subconscious mind will tell you, "See, I told you that it wasn't worth it. Just stick with me, and we'll be just fine." This is when the old programming you are familiar with takes over, and you go back to living the same day over and over again. You will find it extremely difficult to build up momentum again, and you will find yourself becoming one of those people who always talk about what they want to do but never follow up with any action. I'm sure we all have been that person or know that person. The person who says I'm going to go back to school but never does. The person who says I'm going to start my own business but never does. The person who says I'm going to write a book but never does.

These are the people who pick up the phone for their better life and reject the call, who must live with the regret of never taking action and always wondering what could have been. *Don't become that person!* Yes, I am yelling at you right now. That person

50

is more depressed, has more anxiety, and more stress than the person who just rejects the call and never checks their messages. Why is this? It's because the person who knows they are capable of more and should be doing more feels guilty about not becoming more. While the person who doesn't know they can become more is unaware they have become fully programmed. They are clueless about the limitations they have placed on themselves. This person is like a caterpillar that never gets told they can become a butterfly and is destined to live a life inching away on the ground, hoping not to get eaten every day. They don't know they have a choice to become something more. The person who wants a better life but never goes after it is like a caterpillar that knows it can become a butterfly but is too scared to go through the cocoon phase, where the transformation takes place. They fear the unknown, so they don't even try. This is why they feel depressed, anxious, and stressed. When they see a butterfly, they are aware that it could be them in the sky, fluttering around, and living a colorful life. They made a choice not to become more. You must remember that success begins at the end of your comfort zone.

Most people work the same type of job until they reach their retirement age, which is usually in their late 60s, and even when they are able to retire, they continue working because they are still scared of the unknown. They fear that if they stop working, they will start dying. Fear will keep you paralyzed and have you stuck in the same loop if you let it. Why can an 8-year-old learn to swim in a shorter period of time than a 48-year-old? One word, fear. I would define fear as an unpleasant emotion caused by the belief that someone or something is dangerous, likely to cause pain, or a threat. I would define courage as the ability to do something that frightens you. Fear only exists in one place, and it's in your mind. When people say fear isn't real, I disagree. It is real to the person who is experiencing it. The opposite of fear is courage. I'm going to let you in on a little secret. All successful people are afraid. They just don't let fear stop them. They counter the fear with more courage to take action. Here is a trick you can use to counter the fear you have surrounding a certain thing in your life that you want to conquer. Ask yourself: What is the worst that can happen if you go after it and don't succeed? Then ask yourself: What will be the outcome if you do succeed? Doing this will turn your fear down a few levels, and it will appear to you in its' truest form, which is just doubt. There is a feeling of uncertainty around what you want to do, and the outcome is really what it is. If you live with fear long enough, it turns into your own personal boogie man, grows bigger every day, and haunts you everywhere you go.

You must not let this happen to you. You need to realize

you will be afraid of stepping out into the unknown, but have the courage and confidence to push through that obstacle. Believe in the vision you have for your better life and chase it down by picking up the phone every day and showing up ready to win the battle over your mind, because that is what you have to be prepared for — a battle over your mind. Think of positive thoughts as your own personal soldiers on the battlefield of your mind, and negative thoughts as the enemy. The moment you wake up, the battle begins. Right now, you might feel like you are losing more battles than you are winning, but this is because you are going into battle unprepared. I can tell you a secret: if you use it, you will never lose another battle ever again. You ready? While the enemy might have what seems to be a lot of soldiers, you have access to an unlimited number of soldiers you can call on all day to fight. You can send them in wave after wave to crush the enemy. They won't stand a chance. It will be like a thousand piranhas attacking once and devouring your opponent. This is what feeding yourself positivity all day will do for you. If you go into battle without a strategy, you are almost guaranteed to lose. This is why you must set yourself up every day to win. If you win enough battles in a row, you will have the confidence to conquer any enemy that threatens you.

Another technique you can use to prepare your mind to

win the battle every day is affirmation. When someone tells you that you did a great job or that they are proud of you, it makes you feel good inside because they are affirming you. They are encouraging you and showing support. It makes you want to continue to do better. When your boss has a meeting and tells you that you did a great job on a presentation, or your coach gives you the game ball you feel is important, it lifts your spirits. When we are affirmed in public, we feel a sense of confidence and pride that makes us want to achieve more to get that feeling again, but how often are we affirmed in public?

What you need to do is start affirming yourself to yourself every day. Don't wait for someone to affirm you in public, because the moment you feel like you should be affirmed in public but aren't, you get discouraged. If you do a great job on that presentation and your boss doesn't acknowledge it, you will start to feel like they don't value you. When you have a great game, but the coach gives the game ball to the person who made one big play at the end, you feel slighted. That is because you have not built up enough personal affirmation to understand that you don't need any outside affirmation to feel good inside. This might sound stupid or like it is a waste of time, but it works. I want you to write down 5 to 10 affirmations that you will repeat out loud to yourself daily in the morning before you start your day. Start every affirmation with the words "I am." For example, 'I am successful in everything that I put my energy into.' 'I am confident in my ability to win the battle over my mind every day.' 'I am healthy, wealthy, and living my better life.' You can affirm anything to yourself you want. My suggestion is that you look at yourself in the mirror when you do this. When soldiers go into battle, they all put on armor for protection for the upcoming fight against the enemy, and you should too. That is what affirmations will do for you. Any time you tell yourself, 'I am' you are downloading a program into your subconscious mind, whether you know it or not, so program your mind with positivity.

Your mind cannot act on the reverse of an idea. For example, if you say I am not going to be lazy today, your mind deletes the word not from the sentence and says I am going to be lazy today. Instead, you must flip it around and say the reverse, which would be that I am going to be productive today. Whenever you use the words I am, there is always a feeling attached to it. Think about how many times you tell yourself that phrase throughout the day. You say I am hungry, I am sleepy, I am tired, I am ready to go, or I am bored. Most of the time, when we use the words I am, it is not attached to positive feelings. It is used mostly to describe how we feel about the way the outside world is affecting us. You need to understand that you are whatever you tell yourself you are, so why not tell yourself I am the best, I am unstoppable, or I am whatever positive adjective you want to use to describe yourself. Even if you don't believe it at first, once you make this a part of your daily routine, your mind will eventually start to believe it, and your self-esteem will increase. Kanye West said it best: "I use my self-esteem as steam to power my dreams." **You ultimately determine how you feel about yourself. Don't let your success be defined by the outside world.**

What is your definition of success?

Why do you fear going all in on your better life?

Write down 5 affirmations that you can say everyday to move you closer to your better life.

-
-
-
-
-

Chapter 4

Hello or Goodbye: *What's the difference?*

When you answer the phone, you usually answer by saying "Hello" and then waiting for a reply. Depending on how
the person on the phone responds, we hang up or we respond
back. Hello is described as a greeting we use to begin a phone
conversation or when greeting someone. Depending on where
you are in the world, the word hello also means goodbye. In Ha-
waii, the word "Aloha" means hello and goodbye. It is used when
greeting someone as well as when you are departing. In Italian,
the word "ciao" means both hello and goodbye. In French, the
word "salut!" means hello and goodbye, and in German, the

word "servus!" means hello and goodbye. I think America has adapted this to the word hello as well. How many times have you answered the phone and said hello, and the other end responded, "This call is being recorded," and you hung up the phone? Your hello was a goodbye. You just said it on the front end.

When, after answering the phone, the first words you hear are "This call is being recorded," that means a record of this conversation is going to be kept. It might be for training purposes or for procedural purposes, but there is going to be an account of this conversation. Let's be honest, we usually never want to have that conversation because we know they are going to want something from us. We pretty much understand this is not going to be a conversation we want to have because we automatically think this is probably a creditor we owe. We usually don't have the money anyway, so we hang up the phone.

Here is your subconscious mind in action again. Your subconscious mind makes you think that by hanging up the phone, the problem goes away. You avoid the conversation to the point where they send you a letter in the mail telling you your debt has been sent over to the collections department and your credit score is about to take a hit. What do we usually do then? Nothing; your subconscious mind tells you things like, "My credit score is already messed up, so what?" You ignore them to the point where you get another letter in the mail saying you must now go to court. You go to court, and the judge puts you on a payment plan of $300 a month to pay back the company you owe plus court costs and sometimes even interest on those payments.

There are times in our lives when we have no choice but to pick up the phone and take action because life has forced us to act. If you get fired from your job you aren't going to sit at home like you won the lottery; you will jump into action and find another job. Why? Because your way of life depends on it. You are in survival mode, and survival mode is where you do what you must do to get through the day. What I want you to understand is that your subconscious mind is always going to avoid problems. Why? Again, I tell you that your subconscious mind is always seeking comfort and ease. This is how most people live their lives, waiting for life to impact them instead of them impacting life.

We build up these boogie men in our heads and let them run our lives into the ground instead of taking control of our lives. Let's take the scenario I just mentioned about people avoiding paying a company the money they are owed. If people had just had the conversation on the front end, this is probably what would have happened. The company would have said they needed a payment of whatever amount. You would have said you couldn't pay it. They would have asked, What can you pay? I want to stop right here because what I am about to say is important. Please remember this: you always have a choice to decide what you want in life, but if you don't act, then other people get to make choices for you. You can tell them I can pay you $25 a month until I get back on my feet, and you know what they would have said. Okay, that works. When can you start making those payments? Why would they do this? Because something is better than nothing. Your credit score didn't take a hit, you didn't get turned over to collections, and you didn't have to go see a judge. Why? You weren't afraid, and you took control of the situation.

From this point on, while reading this book, I want you to remember that the key to living your better life is going to be represented by one word, and that word is control. You must gain control over every aspect of your current life in order to elevate it to your better life. The reason most people don't pick up the phone and have a conversation with their better lives once they have accepted the call is because your better life is going to call you from a lot of different phone numbers. Some you recognize, and some you don't, but you must answer them all. For example, your better life includes better health, better finances, better relationships, a better career, better hobbies, and I could go on. And under each of those I just listed, we could name at least five things you could be doing in each area to take back control. It's a lot I know. What most people do is live with what I call "settle bugs." They get to a point where, one by one, the settle bugs creep in, and you start settling for things in one area, and then it spreads to another and another, and before you know it, your whole life is covered with settle bugs. You look up, and you have settled in every area of your life. *Don't be that person.*

If I were to give you one word on how to exercise control over your life, it would be through discipline. You must have discipline in order to live your better life. It is the tool you use to regain and keep control over your life. I was once told that the thing about discipline is that if you need it, you don't have it. Self-discipline is the only thing that will kill the settle bugs in your life. We all have them, but the key is to recognize when they are starting to creep up on you. They come in fast and in large numbers. I would describe them like this: Imagine you are standing in a field, and you are standing in an ant pile, but you don't realize you are standing in an ant pile. What's going to happen? You will get bitten by them, and if you don't move, they will eventually cover your whole body. You will probably have to remove some layers of clothing and take a bath to make sure you get all of them off you. The sooner you realize you are standing in an ant pile, the better off you will be and the less damage you will take. This is how life works. The quicker you can realize and recognize your settle bugs the better off you will be and the less damage you will take.

When you see a house and there are cracks in the walls, this is because of years of settling. The house has been there long enough to settle into the soil, and it is now unbalanced in places, which is why cracks appear. The same thing happens to us as human beings. But you are not a house; you can move whenever you get ready. When this happens to you, it's because you have an **X** instead of a **Y**. What I mean is that you have *excuses* as to *why* you aren't living your better life. Your *why* isn't bigger than your *excuses*. If you really wanted something, you would put the excuses to the side and go after it because your why would be driving you towards what you want to the point where your discipline becomes habits, which would then become a way of life. How many times have you heard professional athletes coming from the inner city say I wanted to buy my family a big house, so I put all of my efforts into becoming a professional athlete. If your why is always bigger than your excuses, you will hit your target every single time. I'm going to share something with you that will help you cut down on the time it will take to hit your target. If your why is for someone else, it will always have a stronger pull. Think about why you want your better life. Who will it impact? Who else, besides you, will benefit from your success? Is it your family and friends? Is it a certain group of people you want to help or will the world benefit from your success?

When you pick up the phone for your better life, the person on the other end will let you know if you have been settling or not. If the conversation starts off with "This is call is being recorded," you have settled into life and now must deal with what you have been avoiding. It's the one where your boss tells you that if you don't pick it up, we will have to let you go. It's the one where your car tells you if you don't take better care of me then I will quit on you. It's the one where your body tells you that if you don't take better care of me, then I will quit on you. It's the one where your spouse tells you we need counseling. Do you see how easily the settle bugs can creep up on you? When we get those calls, we can't hang up the phone, even though it might not seem like we are talking about our better lives. You must understand that it might not feel better but it is better, compared to the one you are currently living and will be living in the future if you don't take control.

You must answer the phone every time your better life calls, and you will be answering the phone all day long. Like I stated earlier in this chapter, I know your better life is asking a lot of you, but here is a simple way to break it down so it doesn't seem so overwhelming. I shared this with you in Chapter 1, but I want this to stick with you, so it is worth repeating. When faced with a decision, you must always choose the one that will advance you forward in life. Remember, in the last chapter, I said that growing into your better life will look more like a stock chart rather than a straight line. Here is an example: You eat healthily all day every day and exercise consistently, but today you eat some cake. That decision to eat the cake did not advance you forward and is a small setback; however, you have been eating right for so long that you won't overindulge and can control yourself enough to go back to pursuing your better life. No one is going to be perfect and get everything right every time. You must learn to grow, and the best way to learn is through experience. The experience of letting the settle bugs take over your life and the experience of getting rid of them. Experience helps you realize when they start creeping in, so you don't wait to take action. You act immediately and with intention because now you are aware of what happens when you don't. You know exactly what to do and how to do it!

I am about to give you something I purposely waited until now to give you because you wouldn't have been able to digest it properly without context. I have mentioned the word mind quite a few times up to this point, but not once have I said the word mindset. You have probably heard the word mindset thrown around before, and people describe it to you in different ways, but you still don't understand what it means. I will simplify it for you now.

Mindset simply means, What thoughts are you thinking? Are you thinking positively or negatively about a thing or situation. What is your mind set on? Your positive or negative thinking is going to influence how you react, and how you react is going to trigger your emotions. If you have a positive reaction, then you will feel positively about the situation. Conversely, if you have a negative reaction, then you will feel negatively about the situation.

You will be required to climb many mountains on your way to living your better life. Some you will see in the distance and know you will have to conquer. You have time to prepare yourself for those and get your mind right before you get ready to attack, but there are other mountains that shoot up out of the ground right in front of you, like you are a character in a video game. This could be a family member passing away, finding out you have a deadly disease that runs in the family, you made some bad investments, and now you have to file bankruptcy, or your spouse gets sick and can no longer work. All kinds of things can and will happen to you on your journey to living your better life. It's these situations we must especially be prepared for because they will cause us to settle faster than anything else: the unexpected mountain that you weren't prepared to climb.

How do you stay positive in those situations? When life starts to seem unfair and like it is only happening to you and no one else, I have stated this before, but it is worth repeating. It's all about the questions you ask yourself in those moments. It's easy to ask yourself positive questions when you can see the glass as half full, but how do you do that when you feel like the glass is half empty? It feels like you are lying to yourself. How can a family member passing away too soon be a half-glass-full situation? How can a spouse who all of a sudden is in ill health be in a glass-half-full situation? Here is how, if it makes your *why* bigger. If a family member passing away makes you re-evaluate your health and make some changes you would not have made otherwise, it affects you positively. If your spouse becoming sick forces you to get creative and start a business on the side so you can take care of your spouse, and the business turns into a successful business, then it has a positive effect on you. Remember, your Y is *why* you take action and move. Your X represents the *excuses* you use to settle where you are. If your Y is always bigger than your X, you will conquer anything in your path.

On this journey to your better life, I need you to understand that you are going to be feeling a range of different emotions. You will feel happy about your progress, sad about the pullbacks, scared of the unexpected mountains that show up, frustrated with the settle bugs and so on. You must understand that it is okay to feel your feelings, but it's not okay to follow your feelings. Following your feelings will lead you right back to the subconscious mind you just left. It would be like typing a 30-page paper for school; the power goes out and you forget to save it. You will have to start all over again. You have no choice but to start all over again. Instead of following your feelings, I like to say to fold them up and put them away. The reason you feel any way about anything is because you care. Your feelings matter. I say fold them up because when you fold something up, that means you care about it. For example, when a soldier dies, they give the family a folded U.S. flag. You can look at how it was folded and tell it was done with care and intention.

I say to put them away because they will be needed again eventually. If you put something away, you intend to go back to it at some point. If you throw something away, you don't think you will ever need it again. The feelings you just folded up and put away will be brought back at some point, and when they are, it is because you need them at that moment in time to deal with the situation you are facing. This will put you on the path to becoming the master of your emotions. Fold them up, put them away, and immediately think of a positive way that your feelings can be part of your Y (reasons why) and not an X (excuses).

To help you understand why your X is so strong in your life and why your excuses for not living your better life are holding you back, is because they are probably true but that doesn't mean they are real. Here is an example. Remember the 38-year-old with NBA dreams? He tells himself, "I could have made it to the NBA, but I didn't have anyone encouraging me." I didn't have anyone to help me get there. My environment was not good growing up. My mom was never home because she had to work two jobs. I don't even know who my father is, I was surrounded by gangs and had to fight all the time. His excuses are all true, but they aren't real. All of these things did happen to him, and that's true, but the reality of why he didn't make it is because *he* quit *his* dream. When people make excuses, there are almost always external factors outside of themselves as to why they didn't accomplish their goal. They usually never put the blame squarely on themselves and say the reason I don't have it is because I gave up on it. You gave up on it because your Y wasn't strong enough. At some point, you started following your emotions, and they led you into a loop that took you right back to the start of the race.

If you do this enough times, you will just quit all together, and this is what most people do. They just follow their emotions on an endless loop that always has them starting over and over again until they don't even try to run the race anymore. *Don't be that person.* You must learn to master your emotions and let them go as quickly as possible so you can get back to the battlefield because the battle over your mind is still going on. What are you saying to those negative thoughts? Are you saying hello or goodbye? Sometimes it means the same thing when you don't know whether they are coming or going. You are telling your negative feelings goodbye, but those feelings hear hello when you mean goodbye because your X (excuses) are bigger than your Y (reasons why).

Reasons why you didn't and excuses are like identical twins. They can look the same, act the same, walk the same, and talk the same, but they are not the same. They both have different fingerprints. Excuses can never change. They will always be a negative force in your life that wants to pull you back as far as it can, so you never change. Reasons can change. They can start out the same as excuses, but you can flip them from negative to positive by adding them to your why. You will win every time you do this. When you do this, it's like going into battle and convincing half of the opposing side they should fight with you instead of the opposition, and they flip sides. Let's go back to the 38-year-old with NBA dreams. For example, when he says, "My mom was never home because she was always working two jobs." he can change it from an excuse to a reason why by saying, "I'm going to make sure my mother never has to work another day in her life." When he says, "I don't even know who my father is," he can flip it by saying, "One day my father is

going to see me on TV and know that I made it without him."
When he says, "I was surrounded by gangs and had to fight
all the time," he can flip it by saying, "I'm going to get out of
here with basketball. I'm not going to be like the rest of them."

Your X (excuses) and your Y (reasons why) form your
mentality. All mentality means is the way you see the world.
Are you an X person or a Y person? Do you have more excuses as to why you don't or more reasons why you will? I'm
sure most of you have heard about Kobe Bryant's Mam-
ba mentality. This is what he was trying to get us to understand. **If you have no X's (excuses) and can stack up
enough Y's (reasons why), then you will be unstoppable.**

List the top 5 areas in your life were you need to regain control? *Number from 1-5 with 1 being the most important.*

1.

2.

3.

4.

5.

List **3 X's** that you have let you hold you back.

1.

2.

3.

List **3 Y's** that will pull you forward..

1.

2.

3.

Chapter 5

The Present: *Past or Future*

All you have is the present. The past has already happened, and the future doesn't exist. When you pick up the phone, you are usually having a conversation about the past or the future. Most of the time, if we are talking to people we don't know, it's about the future. Someone is calling to see if you want to sell your house, the creditors are calling to see when you can pay them, or that job you applied for is telling you to come in for an interview. Most of the time, when we talk to people, we know we are talking about the past. We say things like, let me tell you what just happened to me. Did you see the game last night? Did you see what happened on the news today?

I believe it is no coincidence that the words present and gift have the same meaning. Time is the best gift you will ever receive because it means you have another chance to get it right, another chance to pick up the phone for your better life. When you are out of time, that's it. We all know people who ran out of time. One day you will run out of time too, so cherish the time you have left. Most people just spend time waiting for something to happen. *Don't be that person.* The key word I want you to pay attention to is spend. People spend time and they spend money, so they say time is money, but that couldn't be further from the truth. Time is time, and money is money. You can make more money, but you can't make more time. Use your time to go out into the world and make something happen. Here is an acronym I came up with to describe time:

- **T**aking
- **I**n
- **M**y
- **E**nvironment

We have all been given the gift of time. When you spend time, you are taking in your environment, so make sure you are choosing to spend your time wisely.

No one can remember every gift they have ever received from someone. I'm sure when they received the gift, they appreciated it, no matter how small the gift was. As time goes on, we forget things that happened in the past. Our brains are only designed to hold so much information at one time. (By the way, this is the first time you have read the word brain while reading this book). This is because your mind is not your brain. Think of your brain as the house that your mind lives in. It has no ability to do anything but house information. This is why you forget someone's name right after meeting them. Your mind does not think their name is relevant information and kicks it out of the brain immediately.

If you refuse to pick up the phone and continue to ignore the fact that your better life is calling you for enough time, your mind will treat your better life like that name you forgot ten seconds after they told it to you. This is how most people live their lives every day. They have been doing the same thing, the same way, with the same people at the same time in the same places for so long that they have stopped thinking and have gone into B.S. (battery-saver) mode. I'll talk about this more in the next chapter, but you are basically stuck in one spot. You are stuck in a loop where, for you, time has stopped. You are no longer living in the present; you are now living in the past. When you live life like this, you start to experience time gaps. A time gap is when you look in the mirror one day and the future just hits you. You feel like you went from 22 to 35 in the blink of an eye. From 35 to 50 overnight. This is because life is about experiences. If you don't have enough of them to stimulate your environment, time slows down for you.

This is why you cannot live in the past anymore. You must start living in the future. People who live in the future are always creating new experiences. They are the ones that get to experience what life is truly about, which is being, doing, and having whatever you want. It all starts with two words. "I believe." The Wright Brothers said, I believe one day man will fly higher than the clouds. Tiger Woods said I believe I am the best golfer on the planet. The owner of the most popular car dealership in your town said, I believe we will be number one. We could name hundreds of people. Some are famous and some aren't. What I really want you to understand is that you can believe whatever you want. You get to make it up. You can make it up as you go, or you can make it up in advance, like drawing up a blueprint. It really doesn't matter, so long as you really believe in what you are doing.

I need you to recognize that you have time to spend, but you don't have time to waste. If you want to be a dancer, watching movies is a waste of time. You should be practicing and watching videos about dancing and studying the techniques, styles, and trends that are current in the dance world. If you want to be a rapper or a singer-songwriter, then playing video games is a waste of time. You should be writing songs all day every day and posting videos regularly. If you want to be a famous actor, going to the club every weekend is a waste of time. You should be taking as many acting classes as possible. You should be going as hard as you can after what you say you want right now so you can be better, do more, and live your better life faster.

If you're 25 and want to fly on private jets and drive Lamborghini's, or if you are 45 and want to buy 100 acres of land somewhere and have your own ranch, it doesn't matter; just pick something and believe you'll get it. Now here's the hard part about this: life is going to require you to bet on yourself at some point on this journey to reach your better life. This is life's way of making sure you really believe in what you say you want before receiving the password to the next level. It's like a video game. You cannot go to the next level if you haven't beaten the current level. Only people who deserve to go to the next level get there, and the truth is, most people are afraid of the next level because the next level almost always comes with more leadership responsibilities. Now read the last two sentences again, and every time you read the words the next level substitute them with better life. The reason it will be so easy for you to succeed is because everyone is scared to lead.

Leaders aren't scared to fail. They act and believe until they've been proven wrong, and when they've been proven wrong, they don't think about how wrong they were; they immediately pivot to something else and believe in it just as strongly. Losers lose, and leaders learn. Leaders don't waste time making decisions; they jump into action and figure it out as they go. This is how you are going to reach your better life. There is no way around it. You must lead yourself there. You can plan your whole better life from beginning to end, and it doesn't matter because you will have to adjust those plans when you are confronted with new information you didn't have when you started. You can jump out there on a limb and start moving towards your better life, not knowing what to do next, and it doesn't matter because either way you will be moving towards your better life. Both roads will take you there, and neither one is necessarily longer than the other. The length of the journey is determined by how strongly you believe and how you spend your time.

The difference between leaders and followers is that leaders can remember the past, be present, and live in the future all at the same time. They remember past mistakes, so they don't make them again. They stay present in the moment, so they don't miss any opportunities that present themselves. They focus on the future, so every decision they make is the one that advances them forward. Most people are followers. Followers live in the past, waste the present and wait for the future. Every decision a follower makes is based on their past experiences, which is why they keep having the same experiences. *Don't be that person.* Here is where I am going to ask you to revisit your childhood again. You were programmed to be a follower. In school, they didn't program you to be a follower; what they did was program you to be afraid of leadership. This way, you will become a follower by default. I'll prove it to you. When you were in school, how many times did the teacher ask a question and you knew the answer but didn't raise your hand? How many times in school did you have a group project, and you didn't take the lead or even want it? How many times did you hate having to get up in front of the class and do a math problem or read out loud? I could keep going, but this book is not about how schools program you to fit in. It's about teaching you that you shouldn't be afraid to stand out and live your better life.

It's like going to an amusement park and standing at the bottom of this gigantic roller coaster that goes into the clouds, and you want to get on it but you are too scared to ride it. There is a long line that zigs and zags full of people waiting for their turn while you watch them enter scared and leave laughing and smiling. This is exactly what it will feel like when you start living your better life. This is why you get right back in line and do it again, but you start to notice something when you keep getting back in line. When you get back in line, there are less and fewer people each time. The ride gets better and lasts longer each time you ride it, and you always come out of the other side smiling and laughing harder than the last time.

How are you spending your time? Here is a way to guarantee your success: Learn as much as you can, about what you can, when you can, until you become the person you want to be. If you don't waste a second of your time and dedicate every waking hour to what you say you want, you can become the Michael Jordan, Oprah Winfrey, or Steven Spielberg of whatever you choose. The reason some people have everything is because they gave up everything. I am asking you, how badly do you want it? There is another group of people who don't want to give up anything but still want everything. I have a name for people like this; I call them handouts. You can be a handout or a standout, but you can't be both.

Now I'm not telling you to eat, sleep, and breathe what you say you want to the point where you are spending every second of your day pursuing it. I'm just telling you that some people are that committed to their success. It just depends on how successful you want to be. If you want to be the next sports star, social media, star or movie star, then yes, you will have to give up that much and probably more. For most of you reading this book, you probably just want a better life, and you may still be saying to yourself, I don't know what my better life looks like. Yes, you do. Everyone knows what their better life looks like. You've just been programmed not to want it. I'll prove it to you. Let's try this exercise. Take your time and think about your answers to these questions. Again, take your time and answer these questions. Ready? Do you want a better car? Yes or no? If yes, then how much better? Do you want a better job? Yes or no? If yes, then how much better? Do you want to have better relationships? Yes or no? If yes, then how much better?

When you thought about how much better of a car you wanted, what did you say? You probably said something that you see as attainable. You probably mentioned a car that plenty of people are driving around in right now. You could have said any car in the world. You could have said a Bugatti. Why didn't you? Because I didn't ask you about your dream car, I asked you how much of a better car you think you deserve, and your subconscious mind showed its limits. When I asked you how much of a better job you wanted, your subconscious mind did the same thing. You probably gave an answer that you thought was attainable. You could have said anything, but you didn't. If I asked you about your dream job, you would have said movie director, musician, or something more creative than what you just picked. Same thing about relationships. You probably went straight to your boyfriend, girlfriend, or spouse. Your mother or sibling probably didn't come to mind, but those are relationships we need to work on as well.

You think you must jump straight to your dream life. The truth is, you are getting what you deserve out of life right now. You do not deserve any more than you have in life right now because you do not qualify for your better life yet. The steps you take towards what you say you want are what qualify you to deserve it. If you do everything I have laid out and will continue to lay out for you in this book for however long it takes, I guarantee you will have the life you are searching for. How badly do you want it? The only way to get anywhere you want to go is to move in that direction. The faster you move, the faster you get there.

I say again, you have time to spend, but you don't have time to waste. What does that mean to you? You must figure this out for yourself. I can't tell you how much you need to give up to get what you want. Hopefully, by the time you finish reading this book, you will have an answer to that question. Every minute you spend not moving towards your better life, you're moving away from it. How long it takes to get there is completely up to you. You don't even have to go there. You can just hang with the settlebugs for the rest of your life if you want and no one will judge you. Plenty of people choose this option, but this isn't you, is it? This is why you are spending your time reading this book. You feel like there is more out there for you, and there is. There is more out there for you than your subconscious mind can even imagine.

Time is the most valuable thing in your life. I will prove it to you. Other than time, what is the most valuable thing in your life? Okay, whatever your answer was, it was incomplete. Every answer you had should have started "time with..."""— time with my kids, time with my family, time with my pets, or whatever your answer was. Now that we have established that time is the most valuable thing in your life, you should understand what the enemy really wants from you. Your time. This is what the battle over your mind is all about. You have your better life fighting against your old life, and you know which one is winning and by how much if you're honest with yourself about it. You are fighting against all the programming you have been beaten down with unknowingly up to this point in your life. If you've ever been in a fight or watched one, you know that most of the time, the person losing doesn't usually win the fight. At some point, they give up and just take the beating and wait for it to be over. *Don't be that person.* Pick up some weapons and fight back. Hopefully, this is what you are getting by reading this book. Weapons to fight against the other side. I hope you are starting to understand the importance of the role time plays in your daily life and why you shouldn't be wasting too much of it.

I've heard people give long lists of 20-time management skills you need to master or how time management is the key to everything. I will sum it up like this for you: spend your time doing positive things instead of negative things. Just focus on positivity and your life will start to change for the better. Don't eat negative foods, watch negative TV shows, listen to negative music, develop negative habits, and so on. This is why some people find journaling a good weapon to fight with. It allows you to capture time on paper. Write down only the positive things from your day. Journaling makes your mind sharper and gives you better recall of things that your mind tries to kick out of your brain, especially as you start to age.

Everyone wants your time, except you. Your kids want your time, your spouse wants your time, your boss wants your time, the apps on your phone want your time, your favorite shows want your time, your friends want your time, and your pets want your time. If you want to start living your better life, you must start today. You must pick up the phone, make yourself a priority in your life, and value your time. It really is that simple, folks. There is no magic genie coming to give you what you want. There is no wishing well. In the end, there is only you, your better life and how badly you want your better life. **Which is bigger, your X** (excuses) **or your Y** (reasons why)?

What do you waste time most of your time doing that isn't productive

What are you going to do going forward to better manage your time?

Are you a Leader or a Follower? *Be honest with yourself*

Why?

Chapter 6

What Mode Are You In:
Battery-Saver, Do Not Disturb, or Airplane?

I believe we are all in one of three modes: battery saver, do not disturb, or airplane. If we are going to pick up the phone for our better lives, we should know what mode our phone is in. That's a lot easier said than done, but it is a key component to living your better life. If your phone is in **airplane mode** (A.P. mode), then it functions differently than when your phone is in **battery saver mode** (B.S. mode). It's the same with your life. You can't expect your life to function properly if you don't know what mode you are in. Which one sounds like you?

Battery saver mode (B.S. mode) changes certain settings to conserve battery power until you can recharge your phone. Battery saver mode typically reduces your phone's performance temporarily, which means it'll run slower. It automatically activates when the battery charge level drops to the level you set. I would argue most people would fall into B.S. mode. Most people don't like their job and wish they could quit and do something else, but they don't know what else to do. All they think about is bills. Their whole identity is tied to their job, and they're scared they will lose it, so they complain but cooperate. Most people live check-to-check. Most people were never taught financial literacy, so when they get paid, they think money is for bills and buying things they can't afford. They're stressed out all the time, and they don't know why. If we are honest about it, there are a lot of people dealing with those scenarios right now in their lives. So, what do you do? You must get out of B.S. mode by first acknowledging you are in it.

Let's see if you are on your way to picking up the phone for your better life. In the beginning of the chapter, I gave you the definition of battery-saver mode. The last words in the definition are "drops to the level you set." This is what happened to your life. This is why your life is exactly as it is now. Your life has dropped to the level that *you* set. You live everyday with just enough charge to get to the next day. So, what do you do? The answer is think. You thought yourself to this point in your life, so why can't you think yourself to the next point? There was a time when you wanted what you now have, if you think about it. You didn't even know why you wanted them at the time, but you still wanted them and got them. What you must learn to do is look at every aspect of your current life and ask yourself, what can I do to fix my life in this area? If it's a job you don't like going to, start looking for other jobs or think of ways to make some money with another source of income. If there are family problems, call them up and tell them you love them and hope everything is okay. You never know when your time or theirs is going to be up, so don't let issues go unresolved. If you are tired of living check to check, then you should buy some reading materials on how to better manage your money so you can have more money to do the things you would like to do in this life.

The answer is to act. Do something about it. Regret is the strongest emotion there is. Stronger than pain, stronger than sadness, and stronger than desire because regret is the one emotion that is linked to time infinitely. Regret is a negative emotion that you have associated with a particular decision you made or didn't make in the past. You feel it in the present, and you carry regret forward with you into the future. Regret is always with you, and you can never put it down, so don't ever pick it up. If you pick it up and hold on to it long enough, regret will turn into depression. Depression is like quicksand. You better realize you are in it as soon as possible, because if you don't get out of it ASAP, the only way you can escape depression is with the help of someone else. The quicker you can recognize you are in B.S. mode, the quicker you can change it.

If you are in B.S. mode in an area of your life, it's because you have not taken the time to stay plugged into the situation long enough to get the desired outcome. Now you are forced to act or continue to feel negatively affected by it. Whether you are the billionaire who doesn't have a real relationship with their kids or the working man or woman whose kids don't appreciate the sacrifice, it all affects the way you feel. You must deal with those feelings as quickly as possible so that you can develop a solution and begin to act. I'm pretty sure almost everyone can look at their life and find an area where they let it get down to battery-saving mode. They have let the situation get to the point where they need to pay attention and act before it's too late. It could be something as simple as calling a friend regularly to stay in touch, so the relationship doesn't get lost because of time gaps. Or something as drastic as changing your eating habits because the doctor told you to change, or you could die.

Battery saver mode temporarily reduces your phone's performance meaning that it will run slower. This is how your life runs in B.S. mode. Your life runs slower, and your performance in life is affected by it. If you are running in B.S. mode in too many areas of your life, you will not be able to maintain a charge. You will eventually shut down in one or more areas of your life. This is only temporary. It only lasts as long as we let it. We set the control for when this mode kicks in and takes over our lives. How many areas of your life are in B.S. mode? What you must do is start to move from B.S. mode to airplane mode, and the only way is to think yourself there. In airplane mode, you are feeling great about yourself and how you are living life, but there is a mode between B.S. mode and A.P. mode, and it is called **do not disturb mode** (D.N.D. mode).

The only way to enter airplane mode is through do not disturb mode (D.N.D.). In D.N.D., you can silence your phone, mute the sound, stop vibration, and block visual disturbances. If someone calls you while your phone is in D.N.D., then it will send them straight to voicemail. When you are in D.N.D., you are more in control of your life. You are selecting the areas of your life where you want to grow and move forward and which areas you might need to let go of in order to move forward. In D.N.D., you cannot be reached because you are hyper-focused on getting the desired outcome in a particular area of your life. One of the more challenging parts of trying to live your better life is staying in do not disturb mode long enough to see it through.

Do not disturb is all about eliminating distractions. It's about saying to yourself, what do I want to change in my life? Do not let any distractions deter you from accomplishing your goal. If you are in D.N.D. mode, you are grinding, trying to figure something out. You are putting effort and energy into some aspect of your life, trying to get things to turn out in your favor. You have made a choice to move towards a desired outcome that you have chosen ahead of time. You have acted. It could be something as small as looking up how much a class at the local college is. Or it could be going back to college and enrolling in a class to finish that degree you started but never got. You tell yourself I will start with one class a semester. You tell yourself, if I can call myself a college student, I will be working towards a better life. Before you know it, you are taking three classes a semester and another during the summer session. You look up, and now you are close to graduation.

D.N.D. mode is where the unexpected mountain you have to climb will appear in your life. It's what will test you to see how badly you really want what you say you want. One of the main reasons why people fail their tests and end up going back to B.S. mode is because they are trying to change too many areas of their lives at once. You try to live five better lives at the same time, and your mind can't handle that many tests. Your mind operates best when you give it one singular task to focus on. Don't try to change your diet, exercise regularly, go back to school, and find another job all at the same time. This is the quickest way to enter B.S. mode. You must pick one aspect at a time you want to change and focus on that area and that area alone. You must exercise enough discipline to develop productive habits that will turn into a lifestyle of productivity. What you will find is that some areas of your better life will naturally blend together. By picking up the phone for your life in one area, you will also be affecting your better life in other areas. For example, if I start exercising regularly and really stick with it to the point where it becomes a part of my routine and now a part of my lifestyle, but I still smoke cigarettes, at some point your mind is going to start talking to you. Your mind will tell you why you are trying to be so healthy, but you are still killing yourself with cigarettes. You need to put them down for good. It could be food for you. Your mind is going to ask you why you are working out so hard if you are just going to continue to eat junk food and drink sodas all the time. You are defeating the purpose of changing to a healthier lifestyle.

You need to be aware when this is happening to you. This is the moment when most people often get discouraged and go back to B.S. mode after they have made significant progress in a positive direction. You must be aware of when your subconscious mind turns into a hater. It will start telling you things like you have changed this, but if you are still doing that, then what's the point? Your subconscious mind will make you think it is taking you too long to change, so you will never be able to see it through. If you start to listen to the hater in your mind, you will go back to B.S. immediately. You will ignore all the progress you have made and convince yourself that it isn't worth it for you to see it through. Every time you start and go back to B.S., it gets harder for you to start again the next time. *Don't be that person.* If you can keep going and push through, you will eventually increase your capacity to live multiple better lives at the same time. You can change your entire life around; you just need to do it one thought at a time.

When you are in D.N.D., you must be aware of any and all distractions that are coming to change your mode. Distractions are the subconscious mind's way of self-destructing before letting go of control. It will say things like, you can study after you watch the game. You can work out tomorrow; don't worry about missing today. You can eat some junk food; it won't hurt. You have been eating right all week. You must not give into these urges you will have when you turn on D.N.D. They will come as soon as you turn this mode on so get ready for them. These aren't tests or even quizzes; these would be more like homework assignments. If you can complete the homework, then you get to keep your A in the class. If you can complete all these homework assignments, it goes a long way toward helping you pass the class, but you won't fail because you missed one homework assignment. If you miss enough of them, your failure is guaranteed.

D.N.D. mode is reserved for those who have made a decision to pick up the phone for their better life and have the conversation they have been avoiding. They have decided to take action and commit to seeing themselves being, doing, and having what they want from life. It's for the person who realizes their life will only get better if they get better. It's for people who realize time is the most valuable thing they own so they maximize what time they have in order to get there faster. It's for the people who have a Y (reasons why) so much bigger than their X (excuses); it doesn't matter what happens along the way. There is nothing stopping them from getting to a better life. D.N.D. is where you do the work to become the outcome. This is where the changes take place. If you can make it through D.N.D. mode, then you find yourself in A.P. mode. Airplane mode is a good place to be, but it's not a good place to live.

When your phone is in airplane mode, it essentially shuts off all communication with the outside world. It shuts off all signal transmissions from your device. Your phone has stopped searching for a signal in airplane mode. We should all get to experience airplane mode in our lives at some point. It's like when you started that business and you stayed in D.N.D. the whole time, and now your business has turned a corner and is making a good profit. Now you have enough confidence to quit your job. You are proud of yourself, and you should be. You should always celebrate your major accomplishments in life. Those are the moments that make you want to experience your next better life. A.P. mode is a chance to take a 30,000-foot view of your life and look at what you have accomplished to map out where you want to go next. You've stopped searching for a signal just long enough to reflect on how far you have come and the growth you have made. When you turn the signal back on, you know you are capable of anything you put your mind to. You know how to say "I want that" and move towards it until you have it.

The problem with airplane mode for a lot of people is that it can turn into a comfort zone, and now they are scared to leave it. This is when the settlebugs come in and take over your life again. They are always right there, waiting for you to invite them in. This is why you can't stay in airplane mode for too long. If you stay in

A.P. mode too long, it starts to feel like B. S. mode. It's okay to celebrate the fact that your business just turned a good profit, but this doesn't mean you should go buy a brand new car. You are trying to grow a business, not your lifestyle. The billionaire who misses all of the family get-togethers because they have more important things to do. You started doing this for your family. When did it become more about you than them? You can easily go from A.P. back to B.S., and you didn't even realize it happened. You need to understand that every better life you chase down and live has a B.S. mode trying to catch up to you. You must remember that your B.S. kicks in when your life drops to the level you set.

You will know you are in B.S. mode when you start having feelings about certain areas of your life and you either ignore them or take action. This is why you can't stay here too long; if you do, the way you view the outside world will start controlling your internal feelings instead of your internal feelings controlling the way you view the outside world. Your external world is filled with settlebugs. Don't let them in. Your internal world is filled with what's possible. It's the glass half full all the time. The best way to live is to go from D.N.D. to airplane, and then go back to D.N.D. and keep repeating this process. It is best to alternate between these two modes and continue to live your better life again and again rather than live the same day again and again. Stay as far away as you can from B.S. This is why a poor person doesn't understand why a rich person would be depressed. Money has nothing to do with it.

A lot of people reach for and start living better lives, but they can't maintain them. They find it hard to stay there and not go back to the life they just left. This is why developing your daily routine is so important. Remember when I said we are all children just pretending to be adults? Children need structure to grow and thrive, and that is exactly what you must bring to your better life when you get there. If you try to live a better life without any routine or structure designed to keep you focused and on task, your success is highly unlikely. If you do obtain success you will not be able to maintain it because you still don't understand how you are wasting valuable time.

B.S. is where most people will stay when its all said and done. But not you. It is the reason why you are reading this book. You know there is a better life out there waiting for you to act and move towards it. You think of it as a target, as a faraway destination that will take forever to reach. Because you think of it this way, that's how it feels. You need to change the way you view it. Think of your better life as being on the other side of the mirror. If you were to look at a mirror and start to move towards it, then the person in the mirror would move towards the person in the room at the same time. As you move towards it, it moves towards you, and the faster you move towards it, the faster it moves toward you. This is how picking up the phone for your better life works. This is why valuing your time is so important to living a better life now. Ask yourself, what mode am I in? This is the know where you are part of the equation. **Know where you are, know where you want to go, and start moving in that direction.**

What mode are you in?

What areas of your life are in **B.S. Mode?**

What does **D.N.D. Mode** look like to you?

What will be your new daily routine to take you to **A.P. Mode?**

Chapter 7

You Can Upgrade at any Anytime:
For a Price

People upgrade their phones all the time. Why? Is the new one really that much better than the older one? Doesn't that one do the same thing as the old one? We all know or have been this person before until we get the new phone, and we find out it actually is a better phone than the previous one we had. We find ourselves on the other side of the argument now trying, to tell others about how great the newer version is compared to the older one. This is why you probably don't know anyone using an iPhone 2 or a Galaxy 1. At some point, they presented you with better options at a price point you were willing to pay, and you upgraded.

Your better life works pretty much the same way. You don't realize how great your better life is until you get there and experience it for yourself. Not everyone is aware of the cheat code that lies within them. Think of the cheat code as a gigantic wheel lock on a bank vault that only you have access to. **Disclaimer:** When I give you this key there is no turning back. If you aren't serious about living your better life, then you should put the book down now. Stop right here and come back to it when you are ready to commit. If you read this chapter and don't commit to your better life, your regrets will grow stronger because of it. You will know better, but not be doing better so when life doesn't go your way, you will know exactly why and feel even more regret than before.

I told you I would give you the cheat code back in Chapter 1, and here it is in one word: **goals.** Goals shape your whole perspective on life. If a fast food manager never had any goals other than to move out of their parent's house, make some good money, drive a nice car, and have a cool apartment, then they are a success. You might have read that statement and said to yourself, that doesn't seem like success, but you don't know what limitations the other person is working with. They might have been programmed to never believe they are capable of anything more than what they are doing now. Goals determine your quality of life. Not so much as to whether you reach your goals or not, but did you try? Did you give it all you had, or were you too scared to ride the roller coaster? You determine whether or not you are a success or a failure. The way you feel about your life will determine your success, not that of other people.

I believe most people have dreams or have had dreams of living a better life at some point, but they never turned them into goals, so they never got what they wanted. When you turn your dreams into goals, a shift happens in your thinking. You start setting micro-goals that all work towards your major goal. Having a well-defined goal is like having a turbocharger attached to your back. It accelerates your progression towards your better life drastically. For example, if you had the goal of eating an apple a day for 30 days, that is a good place to start. If you can commit to that, you are on your way to being a healthier person. As you feel better about yourself, one good habit will spawn another like walking around the block, and another, like eating a salad every day, until you start to experience growth in your life. If you can just push through the pullbacks and avoid B.S., you will live your better life. What this does is replace one micro goal with another and another until they become habits and eventually become a lifestyle change.

Your goal is like a target; the clearer you can see it, the easier it is to hit. Now, if you had a goal of losing 30 pounds in 12 months, you would have a greater sense of urgency about your journey. You would start stacking micro goals on top of each other rather than chasing them down one by one. Your mind would start searching for more creative ways to accomplish this goal. For example, instead of eating an apple every day which is something you know you can commit to, your mind would tell you to also commit to drinking more water every day too. This is a micro- goal you can stack on top of the apple a day. You know you can commit to both of those things at the same time. If you have a big enough goal, then your subconscious mind will find a bunch of little ways to accelerate the process to get you there. Why? Because you are forcing it to think outside of its comfort zone. The hard part for you is going to be making sure you can believe in yourself enough to see it through. Your belief in yourself will be tested when it's time to pay the price for what you want.

You can upgrade your phone at any time, but you must pay the price for it, and you must pay the price upfront. It is the same with your better life. You can upgrade your life to your better life at any point in time, but you must pay the price for it, and you must pay upfront. There is no way around it; everything that's better costs more. You have the ability to pay for it, but do you want to? Your better life is going to cost you more time. You must pick up the phone, spend time listening to your better life tell you how to get there, and then move into action. You need to understand that if you have dreams of having everything, then you will be required to give up everything at some point along the way. Be prepared to pay this price if that's what you want.

Everything costs, and everything costs everything. If you want a 2,400-square foot house in the suburbs and a nice car with a spouse, 2 kids, and a dog, then this won't cost you anything. It will cost you a price, and you must be willing to pay to have it. If you did achieve the goal of the house with the family and the pet what's going to happen is that you will say to yourself, I set my goals too low. You will find yourself stuck in airplane mode, living with settlebugs to the point where you start telling yourself, I want us to have 5,000 square feet, 5 acres of land, and luxury cars. Be prepared to pay another price for the next upgrade, and be ready to pay in advance.

This is why you must think big. You have to set your goals so high that you don't know how you are even going to achieve them. You just need to believe you can accomplish anything you set your mind to, because you can. You must set your mindset to belief. If they can do it, then why can't you? If you start moving in the direction of your better life, your mind will search for solutions to help you get there. You can't let fear stop you when

109

the time comes for you to take action. If you try something and it doesn't work, you must know this is part of the price you are paying for what you say you want. You can't get discouraged, you can't start doubting yourself, you must believe you will accomplish your goal no matter what it costs you. This is why you see people living millionaire lives, and you want a piece of it. It looks like fun, and it is, but these people bet on themselves at some point, went all in, and didn't quit when things became difficult. You can't quit because you didn't become Michael Jordan on your first shot. When they didn't want to do it anymore, they just kept going because they believed, and they eventually became the person who deserved to live that millionaire lifestyle.

For the people who want more money, you are looking at life from the wrong perspective. I need you to change the way you look at life and money. If you feel like you need more money in your life to do the things you want to do, you should be chasing down your better life. You need to pick up the phone and start talking to the better version of yourself and see what they did to get where they have gotten. More money will automatically be part of your better life; you don't have to chase money. Money is a byproduct of success. The more successful you become, the more money you will have, so don't focus on the money; focus on the skills you are going to need to sharpen or develop to make more money. If you want to grow your money, you must understand that growing money is a skill, and just like any other skill, you must learn all you can and put those skills into practice to master it. If your better life involves making more money, then I would argue you first need to learn how to better manage what you already have. What you probably need help with is managing your money. What you probably don't know how to do is grow it. Learning how to manage and grow your money must be a goal. Read books about money and go to seminars about understanding financial literacy. Making more money often involves becoming more creative around money-making opportunities. This cannot happen if you are addicted to a paycheck. Paycheck addiction is probably the number one cause of money problems in your life. If you are having money problems, it is because you more than likely grew up and became one of two ways; you are either a saver or a spender, and, on some occasions, there are saver-spenders. The saver is the person who saves all their money but doesn't spend any of it until retirement. They can afford to buy assets but are too scared to buy them. The spender is the person who lives paycheck-to-paycheck and wonders where it all goes. They inflate their lifestyle to the point where they have nothing left over. The saver-spender will save $6,000 and blow it all in 5 days on a vacation to Hawaii. They are self-sabotaging their financial growth because they have a fear of missing out. Which one are you?

I can understand why people don't value money like they should. Paycheck addiction causes you to have a poverty mindset. It gets you comfortable with the idea of trading your time for money. I heard The Wall Street Trapper say it best, "If you give them permission to feed you, you give them permission to starve you." Stop trading your time for money as soon as possible. Time is not money, but for most people, money is time. I will explain the difference. We know time is not money because you can't buy more time. When time is gone, it is not coming back. You only get what you have, and no more. Billionaires and you have the same 24 hours in a day to work with and nothing more. For most people, money is time because they have to trade their time for money. If you want to buy a pair of $200 shoes and you make $20 an hour, then those shoes just cost you 10 hours of your life. If you want to spend $6,000 on a vacation, that vacation will cost you 300 hours of your life. If you go around your house or apartment and count the hours you have spent, you will be surprised at how many hours you have spent on things just to have stuff you really don't care about or don't need.

If you are unhappy with your finances, your job, your relationships, your health, or any other aspect of your current life, just know that you can upgrade at any time for a price, and just like anything of good quality, you get what you pay for. If you pay the price for the 2,400-square-foot house and the suburban life, you can have that. If you pay the price for the private jets and the Porsche, you can have that. If you have no goals and don't want anything but the crumbs life leaves you, this is fine as well. You can have that too. It's your choice, but you must understand that life is not going to let you just stay in the same spot. It is going to force you to live a better life at some point or suffer the consequences of spiraling out of control. Remember what I said in Chapter 1? Your subconscious mind is so powerful that it can take over your life and literally kill you. It can have you ignoring doctors' requests to the point where you die and send yourself to an early grave.

The reason some people turn back and retreat to the life they know rather than keep pushing forward to their better life is because they didn't know how much it would cost. They thought they were willing to pay the price for what they wanted. But at some point, the price got out of hand for them, and they decided turning back was better than going forward. *Don't be that person.* Remember what I said before? We all have enough to pay whatever it costs to have it. The question is, are you willing to pay it? Unlike when you go to the store where the price is listed for everything and you know exactly how much it costs before you get to the register, your better life doesn't have a price listed. It's more like the game show The Price is Right, where you must guess how much something costs, and the further along you get in the game, the more the price is revealed to you.

Your better life might cost more than you think it will or more than you think it should, but you have to know you can afford it. There will come a time when you'll start to question yourself on your journey and ask yourself: Is it worth it? Why am I doing all of this? This is too much, but you must remember that you can pay the price because you have it to spend. You need to remember your Y (reasons why) in these moments and put them in front of your X (excuses) so you can push through those difficult times. Your reasons for doing it must be stronger than your excuses for not doing it. If you start and turn back before you finish your journey, you will have to live with the regret of knowing you could have paid the price and you didn't. You were too scared to follow through, and you don't even know what you were afraid of. You'll tell yourself, I could have done this or I should have done that, but you didn't. There are two words that, if you have to live with them, they never go away and they haunt you like a ghost for the rest of your life: "What if?"

This is why I put the disclaimer at the beginning of this

chapter, because after reading this chapter, you should have some goals you want to start working on so you can accelerate your growth and start living your better life as soon as possible. But you can also look back on your life and see some "what if" moments that you are living with. If you have had enough of them in the past, you already know how much those regrets weigh. Don't add more to the load you are already carrying. Take action and follow through all the way until the end, because you *can* see it through. You just need to realize you already have enough to spend on what you want. We spend money to purchase things we want in life, and our better life works the same way. We spend time to purchase the better life we want. How much time we spend on our better life determines how much better the life we want will be.

You can't spend all your time playing video games and eating pizza and think you are going to be healthy and wealthy. You can't go shopping every time you get paid and spend all your money on things you don't need and think you are going to be able to buy a house one day. You can't save up $6,000 for a vacation and then blow it all up in 4 days and wonder why you don't have money to invest. You must regain control of your mind by asking yourself, why do you do that? Why am I self-sabotaging my own growth in life? What am I afraid of? You will eventually realize you are afraid of your own shadow.

You are afraid of your own growth. It's no different than when you were a child and were afraid of the dark. The fear you are experiencing is all in your mind and is keeping you from picking up the phone and advancing towards your better life. The only fear you have is the fear of the unknown, and the only thing you don't know is how much your better life will cost you. This will be revealed to you along the way, but you must remember that you have enough to pay the price for what you want. **Just be willing to pay the price in advance, no matter what it costs you, and you can have it if you want it.**

THINK

BIG

List 3 goals you want to achieve over the next 60 days.

-
-
-

List 3 goals you want to achieve over the next 365 days.

-
-
-

List 3 goals you want to achieve in your lifetime.

-
-
-

Checkpoint

At this is the point in the book I want to check where you are on your journey. Take the next two pages write how you feel about where you are, where you want to go and how you are going to move in that direction.

Chapter 8

Storage Space Low:
Delete or Expand

Most of the time, we delete things from our phones because we are forced to. We will get a message from our phone saying something like "storage space is low." You must delete some things from your phone, expand your phone's memory, or transfer information to an external storage device. If you don't and just continue to use it without deleting or expanding, your phone will tell you it will not function properly, and you will no longer be able to store any new information. We usually delete things from our phones that we know are just taking up space and not going to be needed in the future. If we value the information, we don't delete it and choose other less valuable information to delete to make room for the new information. Your life works in exactly the same way. At some point, you will be presented with the option to delete or expand your life.

Most people are always in the storage space-low phase of their lives. They chose to delete all the time rather than to expand. The reason you chose to delete is because you know you have a lot of useless information you are downloading every day that serves you in no way. How many hours of football or basketball games have you watched over the years? How many hours of soap operas have you watched over the years? How many hours of video games have you played over the years? How many hours have you given to social media over the years? This is why it's so easy for your brain to delete who won the game three weeks ago and what the score was. It's because you have consumed so much of one meaningless thing that your mind has to delete it in order for you to keep enjoying this distraction. You have consumed so much of this meaningless thing that your brain has run out of storage space for it. When most of your time is wasted doing things that don't progress you forward, the settlebugs come back, and you start to experience time gaps again. Your brain will store as much information as the mind allows it to, and the mind only stores information it feels is important.

This is why reading is so important to living a better life. It is the only way to expand your brain's capacity. You will need to become a reader to progress in life. You will need to read to advance toward your better life. If you think you can get a better life without reading, you are fooling yourself. Reading is the first thing you will have to do if you want to live a better life. It allows you to understand what you know and to know when you don't. This is one of the harder parts. For most people who say they find it hard to read books, it is because they have been programmed to be distracted. They think reading is boring. People are buying mansions every day. Do you know what all of these people buying mansions have in common?

Yep, they read. Not only do they read, but they also read a lot. Not only do they read a lot, but they also read a lot about a lot of different things. There is a reason why every mansion has a library inside. They have enough books to fill it. If you hit the lottery tonight and bought a mansion tomorrow, you wouldn't deserve to have a library in your house. This is why most people who win the lottery go broke. You can only live in a house that is big enough to fit your library. If you only have enough books for a 3-bedroom, 2-bathroom house, that's probably what you will get. If you have enough books to fill a two-story library in a 10,000-square-foot mansion, that's probably what you'll get.

Your lifestyle cannot exceed your library. What I am saying is that your mental library—the books you read—will determine the lifestyle you live. You don't have to own them; you just need access to them so you can get the knowledge and apply it. If you can't afford to buy the books you would like to read but you don't own a library card, then you aren't serious about living your better life. There are no excuses for not knowing what you should know in order to live a better life now. For some of you, your subconscious mind is so powerful that when you start trying to read, your mind wants to wander all over the place. If you fight through that part, you will find yourself yawning and getting tired and sleepy suddenly. You can read after you get off work or first thing in the morning, and it doesn't matter. You get tired and start yawning after you try to read, and if you fight through that and don't put the book down, you will go to sleep. How many of you have read yourself to sleep and haven't even really read a lot?

The key to winning this battle is to fight and read yourself to sleep. Just go with it if you suddenly find yourself sleepy. Just go to sleep. The key is that as soon as you wake up from your nap, you have to pick the book back up and start reading immediately before your subconscious mind has a chance to regain control again. What you will find is that you will have a different type of clarity while reading this time, and you will experience what is called a **flow state**. You will find yourself reading a whole chapter effortlessly while staying mentally engaged with the topic the entire time. If you can make reading a part of your daily routine, your subconscious mind will know you are serious about living your better life, and it will be forced to find a path to your better life. You are leaving it with no other options. We'll get into this a little bit deeper in Chapter 9, but reading is how you are going to rewrite the code that is running the program and download new information to replace the old information.

Reading is how you are going to expand past the limits that have been preset for you. Become the type of person who deserves a million-dollar library, and you can have it because you will be qualified to have it. You have been trying to expand without reading, and you can't do it. This is why you are constantly deleting things out of your life, to the point where it doesn't matter what you delete; your life still looks the same. Tuesday of this week looks like a Wednesday from six months ago, which looks like a Monday from two years ago. Every time you reach your next better life, you get a brand new memory card with enough space to hold the information that got you to that life and the new information you are going to obtain going after your next better life.

I think a lot of people are really upset with life and not happy most days, but more upset with themselves for letting their life get to the point where it currently is. This is the regret talking where you say to yourself, How did my life get so out of control? I don't know what to do. This is because life is forcing you to expand. You have no choice but to expand. Even if it is at the slowest of paces, you will expand. If life forces you to expand, then it is usually very uncomfortable for you. If your job fires you, if your doctor gives you life or death orders to follow, or if you make some bad investments and lose them all, life will force you to move in any area you are underperforming in.

You will always end up on the level you deserve to be on. If you traded places with Elon Musk for a week, you wouldn't be able to handle it. Your mind would shut down with all the meetings and decisions that take place daily. You would be begging for your old life back. If you want to ride in private jets and hang out on yachts, then you must become the type of person who can handle this lifestyle. You want to skip steps, but you can't. You can only advance one level at a time, so focus on the level you're currently at. Every level requires that you update the software, but you don't have anything to update it with. You have no new information for the system to operate on.

This is why there are a lot of people who are operating on systems that are malfunctioning because they have not made a choice to delete or expand, and their lives are crashing all the time, just like a phone. If you made the choice to delete, then at least you have admitted defeat. You find ways to convince yourself that your better life isn't much better. If you made the choice to expand, you understand you are capable of way more than you were doing before, and you just didn't know your real limits because you never tested them until now. If you don't make a choice to do either, you are living with regret, and no one can function properly when they are living with regret. It's like trying to drive a car while looking out of the rear-view mirror. It's impossible to do. You will crash every time. Leave regret where it belongs—in the past. Don't keep bringing it with you into your future and placing it directly in your path. You are making it harder on yourself. Stop procrastinating and take action.

You must remember that you can't bring the old you with the new you into your better life. They aren't qualified to live this life, and one of two things will happen. Either you will recognize they are trying to move back in and you will kick them out, or life will evict you from this level and knock you down to where you deserve to be, so they can move back in. You always have a choice. Even if you give your choice away, what you don't realize is that the past and the future don't exist, so all you have is right now. You can take back your right to choose your better life at any point you feel like it. What you don't realize you are doing is giving away your right to choose your better life every day you wake up. Every day you wake up, you give away your life to a job and distractions, and convince yourself you are happy because this is what you've been programmed to do. This is why there is part of you that really wants to fight this feeling, because it's a program you've been running and not a choice you consciously made. Reading is the only way to re-write this code.

What you will need to do in order to pick up the phone and live your better life is find your **pressure point** and push past it. Think of it like this: someone hands you a balloon and says this is a magical balloon. You can inflate it as much as you want, and it will never pop. You start to inflate the balloon, and as you put more air in the balloon, it expands, and it gets tighter and tighter to the point where you are uncomfortable putting more pressure on it. You feel like it will pop at any second, so you tie it off rather than risk popping the balloon. *This is the pressure point.* The point where we are uncomfortable putting any more pressure in our balloon. This is what we do to our lives. We inflate our lives to a comfortable pressure point, and then we tie it off. We don't want to risk popping our comfort bubble, even though we know we can expand further. We let fear and doubt stop us. You must realize you have set limits for what is possible in your life. You can only go as far as your mind will let you go. When you read, your belief in yourself and in what's possible expands because you now have downloaded new information that allows you to expand your capacity to believe.

You are going to learn your way to your better life. Imagine if, when you were in school, they allowed you to take any subject you wanted to take. No math, history, or science unless you wanted to take those subjects. Only your favorite classes, like gym, computers, theater, or any class you can think of. This is how you need to start looking at life. You can take any class you want; you just need to pick a class, and get the books for the class, and start reading. You spent 13 years of your life following their curriculum. It's now time to create your own. You learned everything they wanted you to learn, and they gave you a diploma, a certificate of completion. Get serious about living your better life, stop wasting time, get off social media, put the controller down, stop shopping all the time, stop overdosing on TV or whatever it is you know you do too much of, and start reading so you can get there sooner.

If you can get focused, by the time you have stacked 13 years of better lives on top of each other, I can guarantee you will be financially free and in complete control of your time, at the very least if that's what you want. And it won't take you 13 years to do it. How can I guarantee this? Because you will think of yourself there. Your subconscious mind has no choice but to bring back options and opportunities that are going to move you towards the life you want. Why am I so sure? Because that's what you re-programmed it to do. The faster you move towards your better life, the faster your better life moves towards you. This is why you can't waste any more time. Because a window of opportunity is just that, a window and windows close. If you aren't ready, you are going to blow it because you aren't worthy of it. You don't deserve it yet.

Delete or expand? What you should be doing is both. You should be deleting things and people out of your life because everyone and everything can't go with you to your better life. You should also be expanding by reading all you can on the subject you want to learn, so when you are ready, you can start applying your knowledge in the real world. How much time are you putting into getting ready? If you are honest with yourself, the answer is probably not enough. We need to get real with ourselves in America. We act like the kids of spoiled billionaires who have been pampered their whole lives, and now you expect them to be adults. It's not your fault that you are the way you are, but it is

STORAGE SPACE LOW: DELETE OR EXPAND

your fault if you stay this way. Especially after reading this book.

People come to America from places where there is no running water, where they live on barges of trash, where they'll be killed if they get caught leaving, and you wonder why they are successful not long after they arrive here. How big do you think their Y is? They have no X's. There is no going back for them. If you said to yourself, "The government helps them out when they get to America," that's what a spoiled rich kid would say. Your definition of hard work and their definition of hard work aren't even close to being on the same level. Don't compare your better life to anyone else's. Just work on your better life at your own pace, but do have a sense of urgency about it.

I said this earlier, but I think it's worth repeating. Your lifestyle cannot exceed your library, and here's a reality check. If you aren't reading non-fiction books, books without characters in them, then your life is already as low as your programming will allow you to go. Yes, you are reading, but you aren't reading anything that is advancing you forward. You are just entertaining yourself, like the person who watches too much TV or plays too many video games. It's no different. Sometimes your life might look good to other people, but it still doesn't feel good to you. You can be 27 and have a six-figure-a-year job, read no books, and hate what you do for a living. This person has no goals. It could be the other way around, too. It might not look good to you, but it feels good to the other person. It could be the cafeteria lady who worked at the same school for 45 years, but she read one book about investing when she was 21 years old that told her to put $500 a month into the S&P 500 until she retired, and that's what she did. This lady just retired with $3,000,000 and a pension. She had one goal, and she accomplished it. It's *your* better life.

Right on the other side of your pressure point is your better life. Your pressure point is just a limit you put on yourself. It's a lie that has been programmed into you. If you knew that you could do anything in the world you wanted to do with guaranteed success, you probably would not choose the job you have right now. You would be doing something else. Well, why aren't you doing that? Because you don't believe in yourself enough to take action. It is worth repeating: you are scared of the unknown when the truth is that there is no unknown. You know everything because you are writing the program. The only thing you don't know is how long it will take, but as you move towards your better life, you are cutting down on the time it will take. Be realistic, it's probably going to take some time to go from a Toyota Corolla to a Ferrari compared to a teacher to an assistant principal. The point is, it's your better life. If you believe it, you can have it.

You must think positively the entire time you are on this journey and, really, for the rest of your life. If you try to reprogram your mind with negative thoughts hanging around, it won't work. As soon as you have a negative thought, delete it and immediately expand your thoughts to a positive thought about the same thing. For example, instead of saying I hate my job, change that to I will think my way out of this job. Go from half-empty to half-full immediately. This will take some practice, but it will help you speed up the process of getting to your better life. Positiveness is like gas in the car on the way to your better life. The more of it you have, the further you can go. Without it, you will go nowhere.

If positivity is the gas in your car, then books are the gas stations along the way to your destination. Your better life is a three-step process away. Step 1 is to read to gain knowledge; step 2 is to act and apply the knowledge; and step 3 is to become the knowledge. Do it until you become an expert, and you will be rewarded like an expert. People will pay you for what you know. What do you want to do? You can pick anything; why would you pick to do nothing? It's time for you to commit to rewriting your programming so it brings back opportunities instead of problems. Reprogramming is not going to be easy. Your brain holds a very complex quantum computer inside of it. You must learn how to rewrite code for it before you can reprogram it. That is what this book is doing to you. I am teaching you how to rewrite code for your complex quantum computer, called your subconscious mind.

Delete and Expand

List 3 topics you would be interested in reading books about.

1.

2.

3.

Find one book on each of these topics and buy them.

1.

2.

3.

What are the some of the things in your life that need to be deleted?

What are some of the areas in your life that you need to expand?

Chapter 9

Software Update: *Install Now or Later*

Software is considered the programs and other operating information used by a computer. Software is a set of instructions, data, or programs used to operate computers and execute specific tasks. Your phone is more of a computer than a phone, so every now and then it needs updating, and you get a message similar to this, Software Update: Install Now or Later. At this point, you get to make a choice, but most of us are busy at the time we get this message, so we select later. If you ignore the message long enough, your phone will automatically update. You are now left with no choice. It forced you to update the software. Your life works the same way. If you don't choose to update it, at some point it will automatically update itself. The child you weren't expecting or the job you got fired from. This is all a result of the programming you followed up to this point before reading this book.

You have been pressing later for your better life for far too long. It's time for you to choose an update before the next automatic update is forced on your life. This is step 2 of the process. To apply the knowledge you have been downloading. Take action, press the update button for your better life, and start moving in that direction. Stop thinking you have more time to get it done. It's time for you to commit to going after your better life. If you want a better relationship with your kids, there's a book on that, if you want to learn how to paint, there's a book on that; if you want to learn about financial literacy, there's a book on that, if you want to learn about real-estate, there's a book on that. My point is that there's information about your better life that you are not using. If you said, "I don't need to read; I'll look it up on the internet or just watch some videos about it," here is why you must read. When you read a book with pages, your mind is not distracted by the light from the device you are using, so you are able to give more focus to the pages rather than filtering out light. If your mind is the software, then your body is the hardware of the computer. When you physically turn pages with your hand, it is different because subconsciously, what your hand is doing reveals the next bit of information to you by turning the page, so you are naturally becoming more engaged with each page turn. Like a wizard casting a spell out of a spell book. This is why a person can read books all day long with few breaks, but you must take a break from computers at some point, or you will get a headache. There are numerous ways I can describe to you how important it is for you to read actual books, but it means nothing if you don't take action on what you're reading about. If you don't combine what you are reading with real-world experience, you won't get results.

If you are reading books about the stock market because you are interested in it but are too scared to lose money in the stock market, then you haven't read enough books on the stock market yet. You won't believe you can do it until you have studied enough to build up the confidence to try it. If you have enough equity in your home and can afford to buy another property to start building your real estate portfolio but are too scared to do it, then you haven't read enough books about it. Your fear is created by your pressure point, which isn't real. You can keep expanding; people do it every day. Once you discover this, your entire life will change. This usually happens around ages 35 to 40. You will realize that you have been playing it way too small in your life. You will start to feel cheated and like you've been lied to, and this is because you have been. This is why you see some people who have a midlife crisis around that age because they feel trapped in their programming and want to break out but don't know how, or they go the opposite way. They break out and realize they have some catching up to do. This is why the average age of a millionaire is around 50. This is usually the age where you have had enough time for the ideas you had in your 40s to generate a million-dollar net worth for you.

You might as well install the software update now and start downloading new information on your own. The quicker you can download new information, the quicker you can take action. It might not have anything to do with finances. Your better life could be a better relationship with your wife and kids. You read books about how to communicate better and how to raise children with technology, it doesn't matter what your better life is; you just need to be pursuing it. Moving towards it as fast as you can because you won't be here forever. You don't have time to waste by pressing later. That family member could be gone tomorrow. Don't wait for them to call you; call them and make amends. You just need to take positive action and start moving towards what you say you want. If you want more money, read about managing what you already have first. My point is that there are things you can do today, where you are right now, to move towards your better life. It doesn't have to be a major thing you do to start this process. A bunch of small steps over time, and the next thing you know, you have taken some giant leaps forward.

You can move at your own pace, but you really need to hurry. Don't be in a hurry to reach your better life, but hurry up and get started so you can get over the fear of failing. This is the main thing stopping you from starting. We need to identify your pressure point and push past it so you can realize you were scared of nothing and start living your better life today. None of this will work if you don't believe in yourself. If you don't believe you can do it, then you won't do it. You will quit every time you think it is getting hard. By believing you can think your way out of any problem, your mind will only look for and bring back solutions to the problem you are facing. When you have doubt and fear, all you see are problems with no solutions, and this is what your mind brings you more of: problems with no solutions. Belief turns to confidence, and confidence leads to action.

Belief grows with knowledge. Knowledge grows with new information. It's time to update and stop pressing later on your better life. Get out of B.S. mode and pick whatever software update you want because the automatic update crashes every time, and it is coming. You can't avoid it. I don't care if you are 70 years old or just retired. You will find out very quickly that sitting around the house all day is not good for your mind or your body, no matter what your age. You will start finding things to do just to stay busy. You might even go back to work. Even at 70, you still need a goal. A reason to get out of bed every morning and to feel a sense of accomplishment.

You get to choose. This is the best part. What you need to understand is that you are presented with a choice every day you wake up: to install now or later for your better life. If you push install enough times, you will eventually receive the whole picture of your better life. It will start to come into view for you. When you wake up and hit later, you don't go anywhere in life. This is where the settlebugs and time gaps start happening, and eventually you are forced to move. Why? Because even if you choose not to play the game, the game is still being played. This is something I am always aware of. Either I'm playing the game or the game's playing me, and I don't like getting played.

Take control by taking action and picking up the phone for your better life every day you wake up. Go after it. You might succeed on this try or you might not; either way, your energy afterwards has to be the same. Your confidence level must not waver because you didn't become Michael Jordan on your first shot. You need to keep believing in yourself at the highest level. You must have even more confidence next time because now you've gotten new information you didn't have when you tried it previously. You need to have done enough research to know exactly why it didn't work and where you went wrong in order to adjust your aim for the next time you try. If you repeat this process enough times, you will hit your intended target. This is how you are going to think your way to your better life, and the best way to think is on paper.

This is another very important step in reprogramming your subconscious mind. When you write notes with pen and paper, your mind puts the software update into overdrive, and you will get to your destination even faster. It's like when you use pen and paper, you are creating a closed-circuit loop in your mind between your subconscious and your conscious mind that is going around like a hula-hoop when you take notes. That's why, at the end of every chapter, I left room for you to take notes. Your mind is looking at the pages and sending the signal to your body to write this down. Your body writes the words on the paper, and your eyes see the same words again, but this time your hand is physically producing the words, so your mind says this is important. File it away where it belongs, and keep repeating the process of storing away important information that might be needed later. This is all studying is about. The more you do it, the better you get at it. There is a reason a very big house would have a library, but when you get to talking about mansions, people who own them don't call them libraries; they call them studies. Because that's how they got a house that big, because that's what they do. Study. A lot.

You can't cut corners. There are no shortcuts to take. All you can do is speed up the process by cutting down on distractions. The faster you move towards your better life, the faster it moves towards you. The more information you can download, the more you increase your chances of success. This is why you shouldn't fear failure. By failing, you have now downloaded new information that will increase your likelihood of success the next time you try to accomplish your goal. Each time you fail, you get closer and closer to your goal. You keep adding new information you have gathered about the goal. As long as you keep believing eventually you will accomplish your goal, so never give up on your goal. This is how the Wright Brothers were able to fly when no one believed it could happen but them. They failed their way to man's first flight.

If you wake up and press later before you even start your day, you have already chosen to repeat yesterday again. Nothing will ever change for you until you decide to wake up and press install every day. When you are ready to start installing your better life, you will develop better habits along the way that will push you toward your goal. Be intentional and disciplined about what you want to change, to the point where it becomes natural for you to do it regularly, and it becomes a habit. If you continue doing this over extended periods of time, it now turns into a lifestyle. This is why diets don't work because you can't diet for the rest of your life. It must be something you can sustain for the rest of your life, otherwise, you will eventually revert back to your old programming.

The key is making a choice for yourself instead of giving your power away to the programs that have been controlling you since you were a child. You can be a doctor making a million dollars a year, or you could be working at a warehouse making 35 thousand dollars a year. It doesn't matter; both people are probably running on a program they were given as children. The doctor has probably inflated his lifestyle to that of a doctor. A big house and nice cars are respected by his family and his community, but he is still just like the warehouse worker trading his time for money. The warehouse worker has not realized they can level up at any point they get ready to. They have all the power in the world to create any kind of life they want from where they currently are, but fear and doubt keep them stuck. My point is we need both types of people to keep society going, but they share the same mindset and the same programming. They believe they must sell their time for money to live.

If you can wake up and press install enough days in a row consistently over time, you will start to develop insight. Step 3 of the process is to gain knowledge and to develop your insight. I would define insight as the power or act of seeing into a situation. A clear, deep, and sometimes sudden understanding of a complicated problem or situation. This is the point you must reach. We know it exists because there's a word for it, but most people quit before they get the power. I'm not making that definition up; that is the actual definition of insight. It says, "The power" or "act" of seeing into a situation. When you can see into a situation It's because you have downloaded enough information to have a complete recall of your mind. You are able to access the filing cabinet of your mind instantly when needed, and you have full access to your entire mind and are able to pull out the software update needed to fix the situation. This is why some people are really good at day trading. They have looked at, studied, and analyzed so many chart patterns that they are able to instantly recognize a good set up and make the trade and recognize when the patterns tell them to exit the trade, making thousands of dollars all in a matter of minutes. They use insight.

You can only get insight by failing. Those same day traders failed, and they failed a lot, but they eventually figured it out. You are just like the hero in a movie. You don't get your superpower until you have failed to the point where you want to quit, but you push through one last time, and then you realize your true potential and rise victorious over the villain. So, you shouldn't really fear failure; you should be wanting to get it over with and get it out of the way so you can move closer to your better life faster. Once you are able, put all the steps in this book into action. Your insight will start to develop, guide you on your path, and cut down on your travel time towards your better life. Insight will help you get there much quicker than if you didn't have it. Insight is something you can develop by taking more action. This is the difference between Kobe Bryant and everyone else. Steven Spielberg or anyone else you want to name who took control of their life. They weren't going to let people tell them what they couldn't do. Kobe Bryant won NBA championships, and he won an Oscar. Steven Spielberg directed E.T., The Color Purple, and Jurassic Park. My point is that they did what they wanted to do, and they believed in their next goal just as much as they believed in their last goal.

This kind of confidence only comes from insight, because you might look crazy on the outside to other people until it works out in the end like you always knew it would. Don't worry about how you look to other people who think you should quit or talk about you. You must remember that they are running a program and will never reach a better life. These people are in B.S. mode, and you can't join them down there. Cut these people off immediately. I don't care who it is, even if it's your mother. Cut her off until you reach your better life, then you can go back to her and tell her I told you. Now, I'm not saying don't talk to your mother, but what I am saying is if your mother is talking negatively about what you are doing, and it is affecting your positivity, then it's delaying your better life. You should work on having a better relationship with your mother so she can understand why you are on the path you chose. If you can have a relationship where you aren't following your feelings and don't allow her negativity to affect your progress, that's ideal, but sometimes it does affect you and you can't live your life for other people. Sometimes you have to limit the access other people have to you so you can have enough stamina to win the battle over your mind every day and enough stamina left to believe you are going to win the battle tomorrow.

Insight is going to allow you to stay in the moment and make the right choices at the right time to take advantage of the right opportunities when they present themselves. You can't get the insight without the installation. The longer you take to hit install, the longer it takes you to get the insight. When you get insight, that's the level of not turning back. People with insight are the ones for whom it looks like everything just works out for them. You've heard people say, "Everything they touch turns to gold." The only difference between you and them is that they realized they could push past the pressure point and keep going so they did. The reason you are comparing yourself to other people is because you have settled too soon. You want a better life, and there is nothing wrong with that. When you reach your better life, the people around you will support you on your way. Even if they don't believe in what you're trying to do, they believe in you. It's your vision, not theirs. Your vision is your responsibility, and yours alone. **You get to press install now or later.**

What is the one area of your life where you need to take action now?

What are the steps to make that area better?

-
-
-
-

150

Chapter 10

Shutting Down:
You Should Be Charging

Very rarely do we ever let our phones get to the point where they shut down on us. Battery Saver Mode usually activates and lets us know we are close to that point. We are a little more cautious about how we use the energy that's left on the phone. We usually find a way to charge our phones before they shut down. This is how we live our lives. After you get off work, you don't do anything that is moving you towards your better life and wonder why you aren't living it. You shut down every day after you clock out from work when you should be charging. I mean the other kind of charging. Charging also means to rush forward in an attack. That is the kind of charging you need to be doing when you get off work, not shutting down by watching a game, a TV show, playing video games, talking on the phone, or trying to hang out. You need to be charging towards your better life every second of every day. This is what is going to separate you from the average person. You aren't going to waste any time. You are going to maximize every free second of your day and put all your energy into living your better life.

All you have is your time. Don't even waste the time you spend driving to work. Listen to a podcast about how to get what you want or listen to affirmations or motivational speakers; it doesn't matter. You could learn a foreign language on your way to work if you really wanted to. It's your time, and you can do with it what you want, but please stop giving it away. It is too valuable for you to give it all away every day and keep none of it for yourself. Why are you the only one who doesn't value your time? Everyone else is fighting over it but you. You can't give your time to your day job and the rest of it to distractions and expect to live your better life. Ever. Don't expect it, and stop wanting it if this is what you are going to do.

It takes discipline to get to the next level. It will take discipline to break the programming that you have been running since you were a child. It will take discipline to break the bad habits that are keeping you from living your better life. It will take discipline to be productive all day and not give in to distractions. Someone once told me the thing about discipline is that if you need it, you don't have it. You must have the discipline to execute every day in the same way. Charge up and start charging. There are too many people who say they don't know where to start, and I am telling you everyone that reaches a better life starts in the same place, reading books on how to get there.

For example, if you were planning to start walking around the block for exercise, this is very good, and you should do this but that lasts about 45 minutes. What are you going to do with the rest of your free time? If, after you walk, you read a book on nutrition and health, you would be accelerating the process of living your better life. After you read, you listened to a podcast about health and wellness, and when you meditate, you see yourself fit and in shape. When you wake up in the morning, you pick up where you left off the day before. You listen to motivational speakers on your way to work and health podcasts on your way home. You then walk for 45 minutes, read your book, and repeat this process until this is your new lifestyle. You would eventually reach a point where you would become an expert on health, wellness, and living a healthy lifestyle.

All you have is time. You don't own anything else in this world except your time. This is *your* time, and no one can take it from you, but you can choose to give it away every day you wake up, and that's what people do, give it away and wonder where it went. You must charge forward and move towards your better life every day.

What is the goal? This is something you will have to ask yourself along the way to make sure you are still on track. Sometimes the way you get to the goal might change, but you need to have a goal that pulls you through all of that. Your goal might be to put your mother in the best assisted living facility in the city, and it costs $40,000 a year, but this is your goal. You might only make $40,000 a year, but this is your goal. Because you have a goal and a window of time you would like to achieve this goal, your mind will operate out of this sense of urgency, and you will reach your better life faster. If you have a **Y** that is for other people, it will pull you further faster than wanting it for yourself.

If you believe, you can become what you believe. Your belief in yourself will be tested on this journey to your better life, but you must know you have been programmed to think failure is bad, and you should be embarrassed that you failed. This is why you don't believe all the time because you've been programmed. Keep pushing past this pressure point enough times, and you will realize failure is not a bad thing. Failure brings back new information to install on the next software update. It means you are that much closer to your goal. Get failure out of the way, but none of this will happen if you shut down every day you get off work. If you do this you are deciding not to take any steps towards your better life. If you choose the automatic update, expect to get more of what you already have.

You must do what you can from where you are in life right now. You can't let any excuses you can think of hold you back from taking action. When you get off work every day, there are distractions everywhere. You must stay focused on the goal and ask yourself, is this activity advancing me toward my goal? If the answer is no, then you shouldn't be wasting time doing it. This is the mentality it will take to start living your better life. At some point, you will be able to get into airplane mode and look back at what you have accomplished and be proud of your journey but today is not that day. You have work to do, so you need to start charging. Stop shutting down every day after you get done trading your time for money. Start trading your time for the future you want. You need to stop delaying the process by wasting time and making excuses. Believe that you can do it and continuously take action until the goal has been reached, no matter how long it takes.

Commit to living your better life because you deserve better. You just don't qualify for it yet, and you never will unless you move towards your better life and don't look back. Don't stop until you have the life you want. The career you want, the relationship you want, the car you want, the house you want — you get to choose it all. *You* get to tell yourself what's next, or you can run the program you've been running since your childhood. The choice is yours, even if you didn't know it before reading this book. If you aren't charging, then you are in B.S. mode. *Don't be that person.* If you are in B.S. mode, you are around negative people that we call haters. The thing about haters is that some of them make it obvious, but for some, you won't see who they really are until you start to elevate above them.

If you are always charging, you are never in B.S. mode. This is why reading is the key to the entire process. If you are always reading in your spare time, you are always charging towards your goal even when you are asleep. When you sleep, your mind moves relevant information around the brain and stores it to make room for the new information about to come in the next day. How does your mind know what is relevant and what isn't? What have you been saying to it all day long? Whatever your dominant thoughts are, that is what you will bring into your life.

This is why you must stay positive during the times you experience failure on your way to living your better life. One negative spiral can undo a lot of your progress if you don't correct it in time. This is when you start to hear people say things like one step forward and two steps backwards. *Don't be that person.* It can undo a lot of hard work that went into building your better life. Being positive just adds another brick to the foundation which is going to hold you up once you get there.

The way you get to your better life is one day at a time. You didn't become the person you are overnight, and you aren't going to grow into your better life overnight either. You must be patient and give yourself room to grow. Don't worry about how long it's going to take you to get to your better life, just know that as you move towards it then it moves towards you at the same rate of speed. If you try to get there in B.S. mode it will take you forever. If you switch to D.N.D. mode, you will find yourself in Airplane mode before you it. Make yourself a priority and value your time. This needs to be your daily caption for your life. I will make myself a priority and I will value my time. Write this down on your bathroom mirror. Look at it often everyday to remind yourself how to get to your better life when you feel like distractions have a hold of you. When this happens, you need to get back to making yourself a priority and valuing your time.

You must make yourself a priority even over your kids because they will benefit from you reaching your better life as well. Not only will they get the benefit of having better life experiences, but they will also get to see first hand that if you make yourself a priority and value your time you can live whatever life you want.

If you are in your 20's congratulations. You are at the lottery age of life where anything is possible for you if you really want it but be careful because these are the years where you should be failing and learning so you can live your better life faster. The older you get, the harder it gets to accept the failure that comes with living your better life. You have more energy and resilience at this age and have not let the pressures of life weigh you down yet. If you are in your 30's then give yourself a round of applause. You picked up this book just in time to realize you were about to follow the program right into retirement, but you know there is more out there for you than that. You know you have a better life, and you now have the experience of your 20's to know where your strengths and weaknesses are and where you need to improve so you can move forward towards your better life. If you are in your 40's and up then be proud of where you are in life. You have had enough life experiences to know yourself. You are in the perfect spot because you feel a sense of urgency about living your better life and you know you could have been doing more up to this point in life, but you chose not to. Now you make the choice to go all in and waste no more time to get to your better life as soon as possible.

If you get to choose your better life, why don't you? The only reason you are losing the fight is because you don't have enough weapons to fight with and they never told you that you have access to as many weapons as you need. The thing about weapons is you must pick them up and learn how to use them and this takes time, but you have time. It's just that other people have figured out how valuable your time is, and they have figured out ways to make you want to give it to them willingly and you do. *Don't be that person.* Be intentionally aware of what you are downloading because this is what runs the program.

No matter what age or stage you are in, it doesn't matter, you can have your better life if you want. The key is to pick up the phone and charge towards your better life at full speed like a car with its gas pedal touching the floor. Give it all you've got and then give it some more. You can slow down when you reach Airplane mode. Then you can chill in A.P. mode for a while, but once you get there and not before then. Remember you can't stay in airplane mode too long either. Enjoy your accomplishments by celebrating how far you've come but when it's time you have to get back out there and start going after your next better life that is waiting for you. You have to stack enough of your better lives one on top of the other until you are able to reach down and bring other people up with you. People that wouldn't have otherwise had the chance to live their better life because their programming was so strong, they couldn't overcome it without your help. They believe in their better life because they see you living yours which inspires them to want more. I call this the **boomerang effect**. When you help other people you learn they end up helping you so much more than you could ever help them. This is what we all should be striving for in life. Where we have stacked enough better lives on top of each other to the point where other people are asking us how we did it.

Let's end this chapter by discussing the **6 point scale of life**. Where are you? 1. People who live below average lives do the bare minimum. They do what everyone else around them does and they might reach their better life when they get their automatic update. They get a raise for being at the job for a year. A lot of times the automatic update isn't a good one. A diagnosis from the doctor because you have been neglecting your health or getting fired from your job. People living below average lives just take whatever life gives them.

2. People who live average lives think they are doing better than most people but they really aren't. They convince themselves

because they can pay their bills and take a vacation every now and then they're doing well. They don't realize they are a hamster in a hamster wheel going nowhere fast. They are active but they aren't productive. Average people lie to themselves like they are doing more than they are, but they know they aren't telling the truth. They end up feeling the pressure of life more than the other groups. These people never take risks and fear failure the most.

3. Above average people have a few accomplishments and know they are capable of greater things than they have achieved up to this point in their lives. They look at other people and think they are living better than them so the above average person feels good about life and their place in it. They can afford assets but they are too scared to buy them. They are afraid to lose their place in life, so they are very careful to make sure they don't overextend themselves. They don't want to risk going back to being average.

4. The person who has a good life has taken just enough risks in life to understand they can accomplish tall tasks when they really go after it. They have reached a point where they have attained some status and are happy with their current life. This group could take more risks to get to their better life, but are living the best life of anyone they know. They don't understand why they should risk losing what they have when they are happy with where they are. This person con-

vinces themself they don't want more because it isn't worth it.

5. The person who has a great life understands they will never lose in life, they will only learn. They aren't reckless, they are calculated. They don't procrastinate, they prepare. They prepare for an opportunity which hasn't even presented itself yet and they didn't even know was coming. The only competition they see is in the mirror. They don't compare themselves to anyone but who they were yesterday. This is the person who stacks their better lives on top of each other one after the other. They are grateful for what they have but are never satisfied. They always want to grow because, they know there is room for more growth.

6. The legendary person is the one who has been consistently great over time. The legend never stops. The legend is known for being the very best. The best version of themselves that could ever exist. Very few people have enough willpower and determination to make their lives legendary. Most people will find somewhere to settle between below average and good. Your better life is just that, *yours*. You create your own reality through your thoughts and belief patterns. This book is your guide to take you from where you are to where you want to go. Think of it as a map you will need to reference along the way and always keep it with you. In the end there is no destination there is only a journey. You have time to spend but you don't have time to waste. **Your better life is calling. Pick up the phone, or don't.**

Definitions

Pressure Point - The point where you are uncomfortable adding anymore pressure to your life.

Boomerang Effect - When you help other people so much they end up helping you.

X - Excuses
Y - Reasons why

Battery Saver Mode (B.S. Mode) - When your life drops down to the level you set.

Do Not Disturb Mode (D.N.D. Mode) - When you can't be reached because you have cut off all distractions.

Airplane Mode (A.P. Mode) - When you take a 30,000 foot view of your accomplishments.

Settlebugs - What you experience when you stay in your comfort zone too long.

6 Point Scale of Life - A range from below average to legendary which defines your life.

Acknowledgments

First, I would like to thank God for my beautiful and talented wife Dericia J. Turner who designed a great cover for this book. She inspires me to live my better life every day. Without her I would never have written this book. She makes me a better person in every way, and I am grateful to have her in my life. My children Anthony, Giselle, and Erica. You guys are the reason why I strive for greatness. I want to show you that anything is possible with God in your life. To my sister Candace for editing the book. Without you this would have ended up being a mess so thank you! I need to thank my two best friends Colin and Loyd and my brother Arthur. The conversations that we have keep me motivated and on track. I also want to thank my mother Phyllis Dixon who is also an author and my grandmother Maggie Jackson-Hale for all your support over the years. I would not be the man I am today without you. Finally, I want to thank you, the reader. It is my hope that this book changes you forever and you never stop living your better life.

ABOUT THE AUTHOR

Grady H. Turner III has worked with the juvenile courts as a case manager for over 7 years. He has worked exclusively with repeat offenders within the juvenile justice system, as well as worked with the County Public Defenders Office. He is a transformational speaker and a life coach. He holds 2 degrees in criminal justice and in paralegal studies. He has also spent over 20 years coaching and mentoring young athletes through sports. He is married to Dericia J. Turner and the father of 3 children Anthony, Giselle, and Erica.

LET'S GO VIRAL!

Inspire others to pick up the phone!

Be creative and create your own!

Check out our challenge ideas below:

- Post a 10 second video of you talking to your 12 year old self.
- Post a video of yourself in airplane mode.
- Post a picture of yourself with the book *don't forget to caption your picture with* **Pick Up The Phone!**

- **TikTok** https://www.tiktok.com/@gradyturnerauthor
- **YouTube** https://www.youtube.com/@PickupthePhoneTV
- **Instagram** https://www.instagram.com/gradyturner2911/
- **Facebook** https://www.facebook.com/profile.php?idphp-p?id=61552901770788

Merchandise coming soon on our website
www.pickupthephone.com

For booking

email: CoachT@pickupthephone.com

www.ingramcontent.com/pod-product-compliance
Lightning Source LLC
Chambersburg PA
CBHW060321050426
42449CB00011B/2587